# Literacy
# Teacher's Bo

CW00841210

## Year 6

Louis Fidge

EDUCATIONAL

Every effort has been made to trace copyright holders and to obtain their permission for the use of copyright material. The authors and publishers would gladly receive information enabling them to rectify any error or omission in subsequent editions.

**Acknowledgements**

The authors and publisher are grateful for permission to reproduce the following text:

The extract from *One Hundred and One Dalmatians* by Dodie Smith, published by William Heinemann (a division of Reed Books Ltd); the extract from *Boy: Tales of Childhood* by Roald Dahl, published by Cape, reproduced by permission of David Higham Associates Ltd; the extract from *The Wind in the Willows* by Alan Bennett, based on the story by Kenneth Grahame, by permission of Peters, Fraser & Dunlop; the extract from *I am David* by Anne Holm, published by Methuen Children's Books (a division of Reed International Books Ltd); the extract from *The Secret Diary of Adrian Mole Aged Thirteen and Three Quarters* by Sue Townsend, published by Methuen and reproduced by permission of Random House; the extract from *The Iron Man* by Ted Hughes, published by Faber and Faber Ltd; *Colonel Fazackerley* by Charles Causley published in *Collected Poems* by Macmillan and reproduced by permission of David Higham Associates Ltd; the extract from *The Sword in the Stone* by T.H. White, published by HarperCollins and reproduced by permission of David Higham Associates Ltd; *Facts on Alcohol* first published in the UK by Franklin Watts/Gloucester Press, a division of the Watts Publishing Group, 96 Leonard St, London EC2A 4RH; the extract from *The Eagle of the Ninth* by Rosemary Sutcliff, by permission of David Higham Associates Ltd; the extract from *Global Eye* with the permission of Worldaware and the Department for International Development (DFID); the extract from *The Phantom Tollbooth* by Norton Juster published by HarperCollins Ltd; the extract from *Children at Work* published by the Child Accident Prevention Trust; *Cinderella* by Roald Dahl, published in *Revolting Rhymes* by Jonathan Cape and reproduced by permission of Random House; the extract from *Getting Things into Perspective* by Colin Caket, published by Thomas Nelson; the extract from *The Machine Gunners* by Robert Westall, published by Macmillan Publishers Ltd; the extract from *The Stones of Muncaster Cathedral* by Robert Westall, published by Viking (1991) © Robert Westall, 1991, reproduced by permission of Penguin Books Ltd;
*Macavity the Mystery Cat* by T.S. Eliot published in *Old Possum's Book of Practical Cats* by Faber and Faber Ltd.
The BT Tower, reproduced by permission of British Telecommunications.

First published 1998, Reprinted 1999

Letts Educational, Schools and Colleges Division,
9–15 Aldine Street, London W12 8AW
Tel: 0181 740 2270    Fax: 0181 740 2280

Text © Louis Fidge

ISBN 1 84085 245 3

Designed by Gecko Limited, Bicester, Oxon
Produced by Ken Vail Graphic Design, Cambridge

Illustrated by Sally Artz, James Bartholomew, Michaela Bloomfield, Paul Davies, David Frankland (Artist Partners), Andy Hammond (Illustration Ltd), Robert McPhillips, Chris Molan, Dave Mostyn, Jan Nesbit, Peter Richardson, Martin Sanders, Jamie Sneddon, Ron Tiner, Clara Urquijo (Illustration Ltd).
Photograph, page 40, © R.D. Battersby/Bo'sun Photographic Services.

All our rights reserved. No part of this publication may be reproduced, stored in a retrieval system, or transmitted, in any form or by any means, electronic, mechanical, photocopying, recording or otherwise, without prior permission of Letts Educational.

**British Library Cataloguing-in-Publication Data**
A CIP record for this book is available from the British Library

Printed in Great Britain by Ashford Colour Press, Gosport, Hants

Letts Educational is the trading name of BPP (Letts Educational) Ltd

# CONTENTS

## The Poster Packs:

- support the teaching of the Literacy Hour
- provide a major teaching/learning focus
- cover a wide range of types of literature, both fiction and non-fiction
- are useful for class, group or independent work
- contain teaching notes offering a wealth of practical ideas
- include activities and suggestions for Text, Sentence and Word Level work.

## Teaching and learning strategies

The posters facilitate a wide range of teaching and learning strategies. They provide:

- a clear focus, allowing you to draw attention to and develop key strategies with the class
- opportunities to demonstrate skills, e.g. on how to read punctuation using a shared text
- opportunities for modelling, e.g. by discussing the features of the texts
- suggestions for scaffolding by offering support and structures for compositional writing
- the means to explain, clarify and discuss texts in a variety of ways at all three levels
- opportunities for questioning and probing understanding so pupils extend their ideas
- a means of initiating and guiding explorations into all areas of language, including grammar, spelling and meaning
- the means to investigate ideas and themes, e.g. to understand, expand on or generalise about underlying text structures
- opportunities to promote discussion and argument, encouraging pupils to voice their opinions, put forward their views, argue a case, or justify a preference
- a chance to develop speaking and listening skills, stimulating and extending pupils' contributions by discussion and evaluation.

## Class activities – shared reading and writing

The posters may be used for a variety of purposes in a whole class situation. It is suggested that initially the text is read to the whole class, modelling good reading aloud, emphasising meaning and expression, paying due attention to the punctuation. The passage may be discussed for a variety of purposes.

- The posters may be used to extend reading skills and understanding. Activities may be selected from the text level suggestions for a variety of comprehension activities, encouraging children to read the lines, and between and beyond the lines.
- Similarly, the passage may be used as a platform for developing compositional writing. Activities may be selected from the writing composition menu. These may be chosen for a variety of reasons, e.g. for the purpose of promoting a class discussion, brainstorming ideas, planning, writing notes, etc., for subsequent use in a group session or as an independent activity.
- The passage on the poster may also be used as a basis for class work at Sentence Level, by selecting appropriate activities from either the 'grammatical awareness' section or the 'sentence construction and punctuation' section.
- At Word Level, the passages on the posters provide many opportunities for focusing on spelling or vocabulary work, by selecting appropriate activities from the relevant sections of the Teacher's Notes.

## Guided group activities

The main difference in these sessions is that, whereas in the shared class sessions the emphasis was on modelling appropriate behaviour to the children, in these guided group sessions children are helped to develop their own *independent* reading and writing skills.

The posters are equally useful in the context of smaller group work, following on from the larger class activities. Having read the text previously with the class, it will now be more familiar and thus provide a valuable passage for practising developing reading skills. For example, the text could be read aloud for developing a greater awareness of phrasing, intonation, expression, attention to punctuation, etc. The text could be used for further comprehension activities from the suggestions in the Teacher's Notes, refining and developing children's abilities to use a variety of reading strategies and cues.

The posters may be used to develop writing tasks introduced earlier with the whole class, e.g. planning a piece of writing to be continued later, working on sentence construction activities, discussing ways of presenting an argument, etc.

## Independent work

Independent work will be happening at the same time as the guided group work. A variety of forms of organisation are possible for this work. Independent work may be carried out within the context of ability groups operating on a carousel system, with a rotation of activities for each group during the week, or as completely individual work, e.g. a whole-class writing activity based on an earlier shared writing session.

In the shared class activities, the posters will have been used for a wide range of teaching objectives at any of the three levels of text, sentence or word work. The Teacher's Notes contain a comprehensive range of ideas which are suitable for independent work at each level, using the posters as a starting point. The posters, if not being used by other groups, could be available for reference purposes if necessary. The activities suggested are often not reliant on access to the poster at all.

Independent tasks could cover a wide range of objectives such as:

– independent reading and writing
– spelling activities and practice
– comprehension work
– vocabulary extension and dictionary or thesaurus work

– grammar, punctuation and sentence construction activities
– proof-reading and editing
– reviewing and evaluating work done, etc.

## The plenary session

The posters provide an ideal focus for drawing sessions together. The session may be used to:

– refer back to and reinforce earlier teaching points by reference to the poster, helping pupils discuss, reflect upon and evaluate their work
– present pupils' work to the rest of the class
– assess what has been learned in the lesson
– flag up teaching points for future lessons
– praise and encourage achievements.

## The relationship between the posters and the Letts Literacy Activity Books

The posters may be used entirely independently as a resource in their own right, as suggested above. However, to get maximum value from them, they are best used to complement the work in the Letts Literacy Activity Books. The stimulus passages on the posters are exactly the same as those which introduce each unit of work in the Activity Books. The activities are different, however. The combination of both Activity Books and ideas from the Poster Packs thus provides you with an even more extensive range of suggestions from which to select according to your individual situations and the needs of your class.

The texts themselves may be best introduced and discussed with the class, intially using the posters. Pupils could use the Activity Books as well, if you consider this appropriate. (The posters may, of course, also be used as a focus for small group and individual work, as suggested above.)

When not being specifically used as a teaching tool, individual posters could be pinned up in the classroom as part of your on-going classroom display, e.g. as the 'Poster of the week'.

| Text Level | Sentence Level | Word Level |
|---|---|---|
| • Language affecting the reader | Revision of parts of speech | Unstressed vowels |
| • Events from a different point of view | Revision of making complex sentences | Roots of words |
| • Established authors | Dashes and brackets | Prefixes |
| • Fact, opinion and fiction | Revision of prepositions | Language change over time |
| • First-person narration | Connecting words and phrases | New words in the language |

*Writing Focus 1.1    Poetry – figurative language; Narrative viewpoint; Autobiography; Handy hints for redrafting*

| | | |
|---|---|---|
| • Scripts | Revision of verbs and tenses | Suffixes |
| • Viewpoint of a novel | Active and passive verbs | Origins of names |
| • Language style | Passive and active verbs | Etymological dictionaries |
| • Thrid-person narration | Semi-colons | Spelling strategies – mnemonics |
| • Selection/presentation of information | Colons | Spelling connectives |

*Writing Focus 1.2    Writing a playscript; Biography; Being a journalist; Handy hints on making a class newsletter*

| | | |
|---|---|---|
| • Writers evoking response | Active and passive verbs | Word origins and derivations |
| • Humorous verse | Complex sentences | Spelling rules – dropping the 'e' |
| • Structure of a text | Revision of clauses | Proverbs |
| • Argument | Official language – tone and voice | Revision: building spelling by syllables |
| • Time in a novel | Revision of connecting clauses | Using dictionaries and IT sources |

*Writing Focus 2.1    Using the text as a model; History and fantasy; Argument; Handy hints for writing an argument*

| | | |
|---|---|---|
| • Suspense | Contracting sentences – summary | Spelling rules – 'i' before 'e' |
| • Features of a genre text | Conditionals | Mnemonics |
| • Features of a balanced argument | Note-making | Spelling rules – 'ible' and 'able' |
| • Using humour for a purpose | Uses of conditionals | Language change over time |
| • Official language | Official language – words and expressions | Spelling rules – doubling letters |

*Writing Focus 2.2    'Flashbacks'; Controversial issues; Humour and science fiction; Handy hints for planning a story*

| | | |
|---|---|---|
| • Connections and contrasts | Prepositions and connectives | Roots, prefixes, suffixes |
| • Comparing texts – value and appeal | Revision of simple to complex sentences | Inventing words |
| • Comparing texts – styles | Revision of phrases and clauses | Wordplay – jokes and puns |
| • Features of explanatory texts | Revision of punctuation | Building words – letter strings |
| • Range of non-fiction text types | How words change meaning | Revision of single or double 'l' |

*Writing Focus 3.1    Comparison of a theme; Rules and instructions; Reviews; Handy hints for writing a blurb*

| | | |
|---|---|---|
| • Writing style | Revision of active and passive | Revision of short and long vowels |
| • Comparsion of a single writer's work | Deriviation | Revision of 'tion', 'sion', 'ial' |
| • How texts relate to each other | Revision of clauses | Revision of 'er', 'or', 'our' |
| • Evaluating style of an individual poet | Revision of punctuation | Similes and metaphors |
| • Retrieving information from a text | Advertising and promotion | Word games |

*Writing Focus 3.2    Authors; Fiction as a model; Writing appropriately; Handy hints for comparing works by the same author*

| | Poster | Range | Text Level |
|---|---|---|---|
| **1.1** | Block City | Classic poetry | Classic poet; Old-fashioned language; Point of view; Personal response to a poem; Structure of a poem; Anecdotal writing based on a poem |
| **1.2** | One Hundred and One Dalmatians | Classic fiction and film adaptation | Comparison with a film; Differences between a book and a film; Headlines; Points of view; Characters; Key events; Summarising |
| **1.3** | Macbeth | Shakespeare | Classic author; Reading for gist; Layout and presentation of a playscript; Characters; Use of language; Personal response to a text; Spells; Rhyme; Rhythm and chorus; Recipes; Instructions |
| **1.4** | Diary of Samuel Pepys | Diary | Purpose; Historical context; Facts and opinions; Common expressions; Writing a diary entry in Pepys' style |
| **1.5** | Boy: Tales of Childhood | Autobiography | Awareness of author; Differences between autobiographies and biographies; First-person; Empathy; Writing from a different viewpoint; Biographical and autobiographical writing; Alphabet poem |
| **1.6** | The Wind in the Willows | Classic drama | Book and film versions; Value of introductions of a playscript; Characters; Setting; Writing from a different point of view |
| **1.7** | I am David | Classic fiction | Responding to classic literature; Characters; Empathy; Viewpoints; Planning with notes; Extending a story |
| **1.8** | The Secret Diary of Adrian Mole | Fictional diary | Viewpoint; Identity of narrator; Influence on the reader; Features of diaries; Diary from a different viewpoint |
| **1.9** | Anne Frank Beyond the Diary | Biography | Settings; Characters and relationships; Descriptive writing; Biographical and autobiographical writing |
| **1.10** | Penny for the Guy | Journalistic writing | Paragraphs; Text structure; Differences between spoken and written language; Use of language; Journalistic style; Imaginary and real interviews |
| **2.1** | The Iron Man | Long-established story | Prediction; Characters; Use of language; Type of story; Planning, drafting, and using notes; Writing a finished story (beginning/ending of a story read) |
| **2.2** | Colonel Fazackerley | Poetic form – ballad | Personal response to a humorous poem; Stock characters/ stereotypes; Parody; Descriptive language; Descriptive writing (characters behaving in an untypical way) |
| **2.3** | The Sword in the Stone | Genre – fantasy | Untypical character behaviour; Paragraphs; Main points; Signalling time in a text; Using flashbacks |
| **2.4** | Facts on Alcohol | Discussion text | Features of a balanced written argument; Scanning and close-reading; Facts and opinions; Persuasive language; Evaluation of effectiveness; Composing a balanced argument |

| Sentence Level | Word Level |
| --- | --- |
| Word classes; Connectives and conjunctions | Letter patterns; Word changes over time |
| Experimenting with word order; Connectives and conjunctions; Maintaining cohesion | Prefixes; Word endings; Origins of place names |
| Imperative verbs; Common conjunctions; Clauses | Rhyming (same letter pattern/same sound; same letter pattern/different sound); Apostrophes; Old-fashioned vocabulary |
| Standard English; Prepositions; Connecting words and phrases | Old-fashioned spelling; Word endings; Language changes over time; New words |
| Active and passive forms of verbs; Connectives and conjunctions | Prefixes giving an opposite meaning; Syllables (stressed and unstressed); Origins of names of days, months and products |
| Subject/verb agreement; Pronouns; Abbreviated sentences | Word endings; 'i' before 'e' rule; Common expressions; Gender; Compound words |
| Passive form; Abstract nouns; Significant words and phrases; Complex sentences; Main clauses | Root words and prefixes/suffixes; Homonyms |
| Active form; General punctuation and more sophisticated punctuation | Double consonants; Sound values 'ch'; Common expressions; Dialect; Language changes over time |
| Word classes; Complex sentences; Main clauses | Investigating single vowel sounds; Adjectives describing nationalities; Borrowed words |
| Standard English; Over-used conjunctions | Letter patterns; Common expressions (Victorian); Apostrophes (contractions) |
| Transforming the active to the passive; Connectives and conjunctions | Spelling rules; Borrowed words |
| Experimenting with word order; Linking words | Spelling strategies; Common expressions, idioms |
| Active and passive voice; Rewriting sentences; Maintaining meaning | Prefixes; Using a dictionary; Gender |
| Language features of a text, e.g. formal language; Key points; Note form; Summaries | Root words and suffixes; Argument words and phrases |

| | Poster | Range | Text Level |
|---|---|---|---|
| **2.5** | Moonfleet | Genre – history | Reading for gist; Type of story; Personal response to a text; Stereotypical settings; Use of language in build-up; First-person; Writing a sequel |
| **2.6** | The War of the Worlds | Genre – science fiction | Classic author; Type of story; Stock characters and storyline; Personal response to a text; Empathy; Use of language; Structure of paragraphs; Extended writing (sci-fi) |
| **2.7** | The Eagle of the Ninth | Genre – history | Using cues to understand unfamiliar words; Opening paragraphs; Historical context; Writing a sequel |
| **2.8** | Water Supplies | Balancing and evaluating an argument | Reading for gist; Paragraphs; Structure and features of a balanced argument; Summarising main points; Writing a balanced argument |
| **2.9** | The Phantom Tollbooth | Genre – humour | Personal response to a text; Humorous storyline; Characters; Settings; Playscript; Poetry based on a text |
| **2.10** | Children at Work | Information text | Audience; Using of formal language; Structure of a text; Evaluating effectiveness of a text; Questionnaire |
| **3.1** | Cinderilla | Comparison of a theme – original fairy tale | Characters; Traditional stories; Writing from a different viewpoint; Playscripts |
| **3.2** | Cinderella | Comparison of a theme – humorous poem | Characters; Modern setting; Comparing a poem with a traditional story; Continuing a poem; Writing a review |
| **3.3** | Computerella | Comparison of a theme – new playscript version | Features of a playscript; Prediction; Comparing a theme; Characters, settings and storylines |
| **3.4** | Getting Things into Perspective | Explanation – art | Reading for gist; Scanning; Reading for information; Difference between information text and narrative; Explanatory writing |
| **3.5** | Rules for Using the Internet | Discussion/explanation – IT | Structure of a text; Purpose; Rules; Presentational devices; Inventing rules and conditions for competition |
| **3.6** | The Machine Gunners | Comparison of work of the same author | Character profiles; Personal response to an author's style and use of descriptive language |
| **3.7** | The Stones of Muncaster Cathedral | Comparison of work of the same author | Descriptive and figurative language; Onomatopoeia; Structure of a text; Type of story; Comparing and contrasting with a previous text; Writing a resolution to the story |
| **3.8** | Naming a Chinese Cat | Comparison of a theme | Features of fables; Morals; Comparison with other fables; Writing a fable; Alphabet poem |
| **3.9** | Macavity the Mystery Cat | Comparison of a theme | Character; Poet's style; Structure and form; Use of language; Comparing poems with similar themes; Headlines; Newspaper reports |
| **3.10** | The BT Tower | Non-chronological, explanatory report | Scanning; Reading for gist and information; Type of text; Purpose; Note-taking; Making an advertising poster and promotional leaflet |

| Sentence Level | Word Level |
| --- | --- |
| Adapting and modernising language; Complex and simple sentences | Polysyllabic words with double consonants; Language changes over time |
| Word classes; Conditionals | Word endings; Silent letters; Words ending in 'a'; Word changes over time |
| Complex and simple sentences; Sophisticated punctuation | Soft 'c' and 'g'; 'wa' and 'wo' words; Roman words |
| Active and passive form; Contracting sentences | Root word and prefixes/suffixes; Proverbs |
| Parts of speech; Indirect speech; Conditionals | Word endings; Spelling strategies; Proverbs and idioms |
| Features of official documents; Standard English; Clauses (main and subordinate) | Polysyllabic words; Common expressions; Proverbs and idioms |
| Features of narrative texts; Simple and complex sentences | Rules for pluralising nouns; Changing verbs to nouns by suffixing |
| Word classes; General punctuation | Soft 'c' and 'g'; 'gu' words; Using misspelled words for effect |
| Experimenting with word order while retaining meaning; Conditionals | Word endings; Practising and extending vocabulary by making word and crossword puzzles |
| Grammatical and language features of explanatory texts; Sophisticated writing | Prefixes; Proverbs; Punctuation |
| Grammar and language features of explanatory texts; Inventing new words | Prefixes; Polysyllabic words; Technical/thematic words |
| Differences between spoken and written language; Non-standard English; Simple and complex sentences; Apostrophes | Rules for suffixing verbs; Irregular past tenses; Nicknames |
| Similes; First- and third-person; Active and passive | Spelling strategies; Root words and prefixes/suffixes; Onomatopoeia; Slang; Dialect |
| Adjectives; Similes; Metaphors; Features of recounts; Paragraphs; Connectives for sequencing | Spelling rules; Invented words |
| Conditionals; Experimenting with word order; General punctuation | Letter patterns; Invented words |
| Features of information leaflets; Using persuasive techniques; Impersonal/personal voice | Polysyllabic words; Spelling strategies; Definitions |

**Weekly Planner for the Literacy Hour**
(Using Letts Poster Packs, Literacy Activity Books,
Differentiated Activity Books for Sentence and Word Level)

**Week beginning:**

| | Class | | Year Group(s) | | Term | Teacher | Plenary |
|---|---|---|---|---|---|---|---|
| | Whole class – shared reading and writing | Whole class – phonics, spelling, vocabulary and grammar | Guided group tasks (reading or writing) | Guided group tasks (reading or writing) | Independent group tasks | | |
| Mon | | | | | | | |
| Tues | | | | | | | |
| Wed | | | | | | | |
| Thur | | | | | | | |
| Fri | | | | | | | |

**Termly Planner for the Literacy Hour**

Term

(Using Letts Poster Packs, Literacy Activity Books,
Differentiated Activity Books for Sentence and Word Level)

| Class | Year Group(s) | Teacher | |
|---|---|---|---|

| WEEK NUMBER | Texts: Titles and Range | Word Level | Sentence Level | Text Level |
|---|---|---|---|---|
| 1 | | | | |
| 2 | | | | |
| 3 | | | | |
| 4 | | | | |
| 5 | | | | |
| 6 | | | | |
| 7 | | | | |
| 8 | | | | |
| 9 | | | | |
| 10 | | | | |

# Block City

## About the text

*As well as being a famous novelist, Robert Louis Stevenson also wrote many poems. This is a fanciful poem about a child imagining great things as she builds with her building blocks.*

## Teaching opportunities at:

### TEXT Level

#### Reading comprehension

**1** Before reading the poem, encourage the children to talk about the fun and enjoyment of making things with cardboard boxes, using furniture at home (tents under the table, blockades and buses with chairs), making things with building blocks, construction toys, Lego, etc. Discuss how, with a bit of imagination, these things can become almost anything you want them to be – a secret hiding place, a moon city, a harbour, etc. Talk about the power this gives the maker, too – for instance, in creating different scenarios, and the pleasure of seeing them come tumbling down when finished with.

**2** Draw attention to the name of the poet. Ask the children if they have heard of him, or read anything else he may have written. You might remind them of 'Treasure Island' in Year 3 and 'The Lamplighter' in Year 4 as a hint. Note when the poem was written. Ask the children what they might expect about the language used in the poem. *(That it might contain some old-fashioned language and experiences.)*

**3** Read the poem to and with the class. Where is the child? What does she use to build with? What does she build? In what way does she use her imagination? *(She is in bed. She is building with blocks and makes 'a town by the sea' – with a kirk, a mill, a palace, a harbour, a castle, temples, docks and ships.)* What does she do with the building blocks in verse 5? *(She knocks down her town.)*

**4** Reread the last verse. Is the poet a child, or is the poet looking back and remembering things done as a child? *(She is an adult looking back 'as I saw it, I see it again'.)*

**5** Ask the children to comment on the poem and discuss their responses. What did they like or dislike about it?

**6** Consider the structure of the poem – the number of verses *(six)*, the number of lines in each verse *(four)* and the rhyming couplets, *(i.e. each pair of lines rhyme)*.

## Writing composition

1 Encourage the children to write an anecdotal poem along similar lines, relating to their own personal experiences of building something, and what they saw in their imagination as they did so.

2 Take the theme of memories. Ask the children to recall a particularly poignant or significant memory in their lives – it might be a visit, an event, etc. Ask them to note down words, phrases and thoughts about the subject. These could then be shaped into a poem in verses, or a free poem of random phrases and thoughts, around the memory.

## SENTENCE Level
### Grammatical awareness

1 Use the poem as a basis for reviewing work on word classes. Select one particular class of word at a time, e.g. nouns. Read through the poem and identify all the nouns. (There are many possible examples.) Ask the children to say whether they are singular or plural, common, proper, abstract or collective, etc. Apply the same sort of approach to other classes of words, such as verbs, adjectives, adverbs, pronouns and prepositions.

### Sentence construction and punctuation

1 Explore the use of connectives and conjunctions in the text (for example, 'and', 'but' and 'with'), which maintain cohesion in the text and link phrases, clauses or sentences together.

## WORD Level
### Spelling

1 The poem provides ample opportunity for 'letter pattern' hunts. Encourage the children to look for common letter patterns and to use the resulting words for discussion. You might suggest they list the 'ou', 'ui', 'ea', 'ere' words and notice how the sound values differ in different words ('ou': 'Louis', 'you', 'your', 'mountains' and 'harbour'; 'ui': 'Louis'; 'ea': 'meaning', 'sea' and 'great'; 'ere': 'there', 'where' and 'scattered'); find examples of words with double consonants ('happy', 'I'll', 'mill', 'well', 'vessels', 'pillar', 'wall', 'all' and 'scattered'); find words with silent letters ('what', 'build', 'blocks', 'castle', 'docks', 'roam' and 'harbour'); find words with prefixes or suffixes ('building', 'beside', 'orderly', 'sailing', 'moored', 'coming', 'going', 'lying' and 'scattered'), etc.

### Vocabulary extension

1 Are there any examples of old-fashioned words or language in the poem? List these and suggest more modern words for them. (For example, 'others go roam', 'kirk' and 'Hark to the song'.) Help the children to understand that some words and expressions change over time and some words fall out of use (e.g. words such as 'hark'). Find other examples of books or poems written some time ago. List and discuss any old-fashioned words discovered.

### Related texts:

'Treasure Island' by R. L. Stevenson

Other 'memory' poems:

'Past and Present' by Thomas Hood (begins 'I remember, I remember …')

'Young' by Anne Sexton (memories of childhood)

'First Day at School' by Roger McGough

# One Hundred and One Dalmatians

## About the text

*This is an extract from the well-known Dodie Smith book, which has been made even more popular by the Walt Disney cartoon.*

**Key Stage 2**
Literacy Poster Pack 6

**Letts** EDUCATIONAL

### One Hundred and One Dalmatians

*When the Dalmatian puppies are stolen, all the dogs in London and the east of England 'talk' to each other by barking messages. This is called the 'twilight barking'. In this way they are able to find the puppies and tell the puppies' parents.*

"Take care of yourself," barked the Sheepdog. "Remember those Baddun brothers are villains."

The cat clawed her way down, backwards, to the ground, then hurried through the overgrown shrubbery. Soon she came to an old brick wall which enclosed a stable-yard. From behind the wall came whimperings and snufflings. She leapt on top of the wall and looked down.

The next second, one of the Baddun brothers saw her and threw a stone at her. She dodged it, jumped from the wall, and ran for her life. In two minutes she was safely back with the Sheepdog.

"They're there!" she said, triumphantly. "The place is *seething* with Dalmatian puppies!"

The Sheepdog was a formidable Twilight Barker. Tonight, with the most important news in Dogdom to send out, he surpassed himself. And so the message travelled, by way of farm dogs and house dogs, great dogs and small dogs. Sometimes a bark would carry half a mile or more, sometimes it would only need to carry a few yards. One sharp-eared Cairn saved the chain from breaking by picking up a bark from nearly a mile away, and then almost bursting herself getting it on to the dog next door. Across miles and miles of country, across miles and miles of suburbs, across a network of London streets the chain held firm; from the depths of Suffolk to the top of Primrose Hill – where Pongo and Missis, still as statues, stood listening, listening.

"Puppies found in lonely house. S.O.S. on old bone –" Missis could not take it all in. But Pongo missed nothing. There were instructions for reaching the village, suggestions for the journey, offers of hospitality on the way. And the dog chain was standing by to take a message back to the pups – the Sheepdog would bark it over the wall in the dead of night.

At first Missis was too excited to think of anything to say, but Pongo barked clearly: "Tell them we're coming! Tell them we start tonight! Tell them to be brave!"

Then Missis found her voice: "Give them all our love! Tell Patch to take care of the Cadpig! Tell Lucky not to be too daring! Tell Roly Poly to keep out of mischief!" She would have sent a message to every one of the fifteen pups if Pongo had not whispered: "That's enough, dear. We mustn't make it too complicated. Let the Great Dane start work now."

So they signed off and there was a sudden silence. And then, though not quite so loudly, they heard the Great Dane again. But this time he was not barking towards them. What they heard was their message, starting on its way to Suffolk.

*Dodie Smith*

© Letts Educational 1998

*See Letts Literacy Activity Book 6* page 8

---

# Teaching opportunities at:

## TEXT Level

### Reading comprehension

**1** Ask the children if they have ever read the book, or seen the film or video. Encourage them to share their accounts of the key points in the story. Discuss how animals really communicate. *(Through sounds like barking and through actions like tail-wagging.)* Ask the children to think of other books or films in which animals communicate with each other. *(In particular, there are many Disney animated films the children might suggest which use anthropomorphic animals.)*

**2** Read the introduction to the class to set the scene before reading the whole passage together.

**3** Ask the children to summarise in one or two sentences or phrases the main gist of the passage. *(For example, the cat finds the missing puppies – she tells the dogs – they 'chain bark' the message back to Pongo and Missis.)* Perhaps they could try to do this by using newspaper-style headlines, for instance, 'Stolen puppies located! Parents alerted by twilight barking'.

**4** How is it possible to tell that this story is told from a dog's point of view? *(The main characters are all dogs. The story explains how the dogs felt, how they communicated and how they acted.)*

**5** What can be learned about the following characters from the text: Sheepdog, the Baddun brothers, Missis, Pongo and Lucky? *(Answers will depend on the children's interpretation.)*

**6** Where were the puppies being held prisoner? *(In an old stable-yard.)* Where were Missis and Pongo? *(At Primrose Hill, London.)*

**7** Ask the children to explain how 'twilight barking' works. *(By a chain of dogs barking the message from one to the next, to the next, etc.)*

**8** From the text, what can be learned about Pongo and Missis' immediate plans? *(They are going to the rescue of the puppies.)*

**9** Discuss the differences between reading the book and seeing the film. *(For example, being able to see the setting, losing the narrator, having to use the imagination more, etc.)*

## Writing composition

**1** With the class, map out and trace, in note form on the board, the key events of the story. *(For example, cat finds the puppies – Sheepdog begins the twilight barking chain – many dogs help keep the message moving – Pongo and Missis receive the news – they send a message back to tell the puppies they are coming to the rescue – the dogs begin to pass the message back.)* Ask the children to use the notes to write a summary of the passage in a given number of words, say 150, fleshing out the notes into proper sentences.

## SENTENCE Level
### Grammatical awareness

**1** Choose a selection of sentences from the text and then ask the children to re-express each sentence by changing the word order, yet trying to maintain its meaning. Allow the children to introduce new words as necessary or to leave words out. *(For example, 'From behind the wall came whimperings and snufflings' could be rewritten as 'Whimperings and snufflings came from behind the wall'.)*

### Sentence construction and punctuation

**1** Look for connectives and conjunctions in the text which maintain cohesion and link phrases, clauses or sentences together. *('Soon she came to an old brickwall', 'The next second, one… ', 'Missis was too excited to think of anything to say, but Pongo… ', etc.)*

## WORD Level
### Spelling

**1** Look at the words 'surpassed' and 'suburbs' in the text. Look up their meanings in a dictionary. Work out the meaning of each prefix. *('Sur' means 'over', 'above' or 'beyond'; 'sub' means 'under' or 'beneath'.)* Find other words in the dictionary with the same prefixes and make a list.

**2** Extend this to work on other prefixes such as 'bi-', 'in-', 'im-', 'prim-', 'ex-', 'tele-', and 'con-' by carrying out the same activity. *('Bi' means 'two'; 'in' means 'in' or 'towards'; 'im' is a variant of 'in'; 'prim' means 'first'; 'ex' means 'out of'; 'tele' means 'over a distance'; and 'con' means 'with'.)*

**3** Look for words in the text with the following common word endings: '-ain', '-ery', '-ant', '-ent', '-able', '-dom', '-age', '-tion', '-ence' and '-ight'. *('-ain': 'villain', 'chain', 'again'; '-ery': 'shrubbery'; '-ant': 'important'; '-ent': 'parent', 'sent'; '-able': 'stable', 'formidable'; '-dom': 'Dogdom'; '-age': 'message', 'village'; '-tion': 'Dalmation', 'instruction', 'suggestion'; '-ence': 'silence'; '-ight': 'twilight', 'tonight', 'night'.)* Ask the children to think of at least two other words for each of the same endings. Compare their lists and draw up a more comprehensive class list for spelling practice.

## Vocabulary extension

**1** Place names make an interesting study. 'London' derives from the Roman 'Londinium'. Are there any other Roman place names? *(There are many throughout the UK.)* The puppies were being kept in Suffolk. Are there any other places ending in '-folk'? *(There are many possible answers.)* Primrose Hill, which is mentioned in the text, was probably originally named for obvious reasons. Are there any such place names near you? Here are some Viking words and their meanings: 'wick' – 'village'; 'beck' – 'a brook'; 'by' – 'a town'. Use an atlas to look up place names that contain any of the Viking words, e.g. 'Keswick' and 'Grimsby', etc.

### Related texts:

Ravette Publishing has produced the following Walt Disney stories in comic strip format:

'Pinnochio'
'Jungle Book'
'Beauty and the Beast'

Origin of town names from Roman times:
'Roman Britain' by Martin O'Connell

# Macbeth

## *About the text*

*This extract from Macbeth features the witches' scene and is set out as a playscript.*

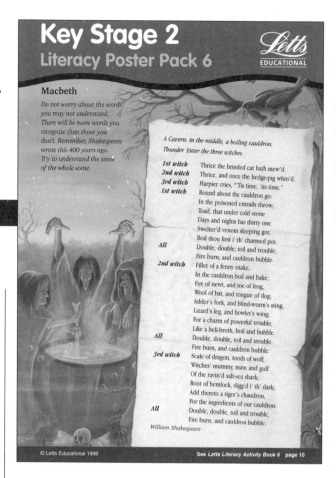

## Teaching opportunities at:

### TEXT Level
### *Reading comprehension*

**1** Look at the title, introduction and name of the author at the foot of the text. Ask the children if they have heard of William Shakespeare before. Tell them a little about his works and his continuing influence, and the fact that his plays are still regularly performed today, have been made into films and are studied all over the world. He is probably one of the best-known authors of all time. Explain that his work is usually intended for older readers. Stress the point that it was written 400 or so years ago and therefore some of the language is archaic and difficult to understand.

**2** Read the text to and with the class several times. Ask the children for the gist of the text. *(The three witches are working a spell.)*

**3** Focus on the layout and presentation. How is it possible to tell it is a play? *(The dialogue has no speech marks and is always preceded by the name of the character who is speaking. There are also stage directions.)* What is the setting? *(A cavern.)* Who are the characters? *(The three witches.)* What are they doing? *(Preparing a spell.)*

**4** Which part of the text is the actual spell? How is it possible to tell? *(The chorus is the actual spell as the other spoken text lists the ingredients to go in the cauldron.)* Point out the rhythm and rhyming elements of the extract.

**5** Which part is repeated by all three witches? *(The part labelled 'All'.)*

**6** Discuss some of the ingredients of the spell. How many are understandable? Which are the most repulsive? *(There are many possible answers.)*

**7** What would the overall impact of this scene have been on audiences? Why? How has the author achieved this? *(The children will come up with many ideas for this but, in general, the impact would have been one of evil and fear generated by the detailed list of horrible ingredients and the scary appearance of the witches.)*

**8** Ask the children for their responses to the text. Encourage them to share their views and to respond to and build on the views of others.

## Writing composition

**1** This text inevitably stimulates work on spells. Children could use the format of the spell in the play as a model to write their own, building in rhyming, rhythm and a chorus.

**2** Give the children a more detailed framework for writing a different spell. Outline that it is 'A spell for… '; the ingredients; the preparation and method; cooking time, etc.

**3** Children could be asked to write recipes (rather than a spell) for real or make-believe things, such as a 'Recipe for a greener world', 'For happiness' ('take a slice of sunshine, add a pinch of breeze…'), etc.

## SENTENCE Level
### Grammatical awareness

**1** The spell is written as a set of instructions. Find the verbs and discuss the fact that they are written in the imperative *(like commands or orders)* and in the second-person, addressing 'you' *(or 'thou' as it was then written)*. *(The verbs are: 'mew'd', 'whin'd', 'cries', 'go', 'throw', 'swelter'd', 'sleeping', 'got', 'boil', 'toil', 'burn', 'bubble', 'bake', 'digg'd' and 'add'.)* Find and read recipes in other books and identify the imperative verbs in them, too.

### Sentence construction and punctuation

**1** Notice how frequently the conjunction 'and' is written in lists and for joining sentences together. *(There are many examples in the text.)* Provide the children with a list of common conjunctions and ask them to make up sentences containing them. *(For example, 'and', 'but', 'because', 'however', 'until', 'so', etc.)* How many clauses does each sentence have?

## WORD Level
### Spelling

**1** Write out the pairs of rhyming words from the spell. *('Go/throw', 'stone/one', 'got/pot', 'trouble/bubble', 'snake/bake', 'frog/dog', 'sting/wing', 'wolf/gulf', 'shark/dark' and 'chaudron/cauldron'.)* Which contain the same letter patterns? *('Stone/one', 'got/pot', 'snake/bake', 'frog/dog', 'sting/wing', 'shark/dark' and 'chaudron/cauldron'.)* Which rhyme but have different letter patterns? *('Go/throw', 'trouble/bubble', and 'wolf/gulf'.)* Give the children the following words from the text: 'word', 'wrote', 'sense', 'scene', 'whole', 'witch', 'thrice', 'cries', 'round', 'night', 'boil', 'fire', 'burn', 'fork' and 'root'. Ask them to try and think of rhyming words that have the same letter pattern and a different letter pattern for each word.

### Vocabulary extension

**1** Find and write the words that contain apostrophes used for contraction. *('Mew'd', 'whin'd', ''tis', 'swelter'd', 'i'', 'th'', 'ravin'd', 'digg'd'.)* Through discussion, try to work out the missing letter in each case. Write the words in full. *('Mewed', 'whined', 'it is', 'sweltered', 'in', 'the', 'ravined', 'digged'. Point out that 'digged' is not a form used today.)*

**2** List words that are unfamiliar. Through discussion, use of context and dictionary, try to discover the meaning of as many as possible. Which of these words are old words, rarely used today? *(There are many possible examples.)*

### Related texts:

'Shakespeare's Theatre' by Jacqueline Morley and John James
'Tales from Shakespeare' by Charles and Mary Lamb
'Illustrated Tales from Shakespeare' by Charles and Mary Lamb

Modern witch story:
'The Witches' by Roald Dahl

# Diary of Samuel Pepys

## *About the text*

*This extract from Pepys' diary graphically describes the Great Fire of London in 1666.*

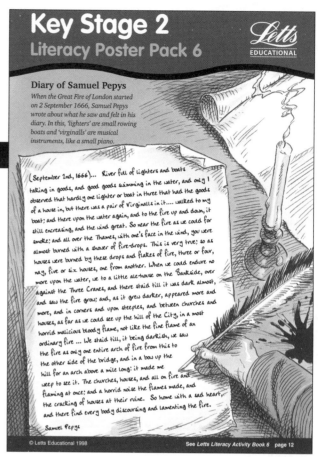

**Key Stage 2**
Literacy Poster Pack 6
*Letts* EDUCATIONAL

**Diary of Samuel Pepys**
*When the Great Fire of London started on 2 September 1666, Samuel Pepys wrote about what he saw and felt in his diary. In this, 'lighters' are small rowing boats and 'virginalls' are musical instruments, like a small piano.*

(September 2nd, 1666)... River full of lighters and boats taking in goods, and good goods swimming in the water, and only I observed that hardly one lighter or boat in three that had the goods of a house in, but there was a pair of Virginalls in it.... walked to my boat; and there upon the water again, and to the fire up and down, it still encreasing, and the wind great. So near the fire as we could for smoke; and all over the Thames, with one's face in the wind, you were almost burned with a shower of fire-drops. This is very true; so as houses were burned by these drops and flakes of fire, three or four, nay, five or six houses, one from another. When we could endure no more upon the water, we to a little ale-house on the Bankside, over against the Three Cranes, and there staid till it was dark almost, and saw the fire grow; and, as it grew darker, appeared more and more, and in corners and upon steeples, and between churches and houses, as far as we could see up the hill of the City, in a most horrid malicious bloody flame, not like the fine flame of an ordinary fire ... We staid till, it being darkish, we saw the fire as only one entire arch of fire from this to the other side of the bridge, and in a bow up the hill for an arch above a mile long: it made me weep to see it. The churches, houses, and all on fire and flaming at once; and a horrid noise the flames made, and the cracking of houses at their ruine. So home with a sad heart, and there find every body discoursing and lamenting the fire.

Samuel Pepys

© Letts Educational 1998     See *Letts Literacy Activity Book 6* page 12

## Teaching opportunities at:

### TEXT Level
### *Reading comprehension*

**1** Ask the children if any of them keep diaries, and if so, why. Discuss the different reasons why people keep diaries. *(For example, for writing down their secret and personal thoughts; for recording events and observations; for reminding them of appointments and things to do – birthdays, meetings, trips, etc., and so on.)*

**2** Explain that some diaries written in the past have proved fascinating for the light they shed on events, customs and life of the period. We know a great deal about the Great Fire of London because of Samuel Pepys' diary.

**3** Before reading the extract, ask the children what clues there are from the illustration that the diary was written over three hundred years ago. *(The candle and the quill pen.)*

**4** Read the diary extract a couple of times to and with the class. Ask the children for their immediate response to the extract. What things stood out for them?

**5** What was the weather like that day? *(It was very windy.)* Why would that make the fire spread? *(Wind fans the flames and causes fire to 'jump' from building to building.)*

**6** Pepys remarks especially on the number of people trying to save their 'virginalls'. Why do the children think this might be? *(As the introduction notes, a virginall is a small piano-like instrument. Point out that spelling was more flexible then, and that the modern day spelling is 'virginal'. Answers will depend on the children's interpretations.)*

**7** How can you tell Pepys was watching the fire with others? *(He refers to 'we' a number of times.)*

**8** Describe some of the things Pepys saw, heard and felt. *(There are many possible answers.)*

**9** Ask the children to try to explain what the last sentence means. *(Everybody is very sad about the destruction by the fire and they are all talking about it.)*

**10** Pepys expresses things in an unfamiliar way, e.g. 'we to a little ale-house'. Select some of these sentences and ask the children to suggest why they sound so strange to our ears today.

**11** Encourage the children to consider the difference between fact and fiction. Find some of the facts Pepys states and some personal opinions he expresses. *(There are many possible examples.)*

## Writing composition

**1** Discuss with the children other things that Samuel Pepys might have seen and written about. *(For example, the Great Plague, the rebuilding of London – Sir Christopher Wren's St Paul's Cathedral, etc. – a royal procession – a ride down the Thames – a visit to the Globe Theatre – a dinner party, and so on.)* If appropriate, let the children research information books of the time to gather authentic details. Brainstorm ideas for the chosen topics and note them down. Ask the children to write up a diary entry for one of the events, attempting to echo Pepys' style.

## SENTENCE Level
### Grammatical awareness

**1** Pepys' style of writing is not standard English as we know it today, as he misses out verbs, drifts from first- to second-person, etc. Ask the children to rewrite parts of the extract as they might be written today. Compare and discuss the differences.

**2** Hold a 'preposition-spotting' contest. See who can find the most in the extract. *(For example, 'to', 'in', 'up', and so on.)*

### Sentence construction and punctuation

**1** The passage is full of connecting words and phrases, linking the account together, such as 'and there upon…', etc. Identify some of these and draw attention to how they are used to link together sequences of events.

## WORD Level
### Spelling

**1** List all the words that are spelled differently from the way we spell them today. Write today's spelling next to each. *('Virginall/ virginal', 'encreasing/increasing', 'staid/stayed', 'ruine/ruin' and 'discoursing/discussing'.)*

**2** Ask the children to find words in the extract containing the common word endings '-ious', '-ish', '-ary', '-dge', '-al', '-ment', '-ure'. *('-ious': 'malicious'; '-ish': 'darkish'; '-ary': 'diary', 'ordinary'; '-dge': 'bridge'; '-al': 'musical'; '-ment': 'instrument'; '-ure': 'endure'.)* Ask the children to suggest and list other words ending in the same way as each of the above.

### Vocabulary extension

**1** Ask the children to find some words in other books which are not used much today. List them and ask the children to write their own definitions for them. They should then check their definitions in a dictionary.

**2** Ask the children to suggest words which have recently entered our language, such as 'trainers', 'wheelie-bin', 'astronaut', 'video', 'computer', etc. Discuss why new words are needed and why some words die out.

### Related texts:

Other diarists:

'The Diary of Anne Frank' by Anne Frank

Research books for finding out about London's buildings:

'How They Were Built' by David J. Brown (information on Tower of London, Old London Bridge)

'The Fantastic Cutaway Book of Giant Buildings' by J. Kirkwood

Books on the Plague and the Great Fire:

'All About the Great Plague' by Pam Robson
'The Plague and Fire' by Rhoda Nottridge

# Boy: Tales of Childhood

## *About the text*

*This is an extract from an autobiographical account by Roald Dahl, of his time at boarding school as a nine-year-old child.*

## Teaching opportunities at:

### TEXT Level
### *Reading comprehension*

1 Read the introduction and look at the illustration with the children. How is it possible to tell Roald Dahl is writing about his childhood? *(Use the word 'autobiography' to describe the passage. Explain the difference between this and a biography.)* Ask the children what other books they know by Roald Dahl.

2 Discuss how they might feel if they were sent away from their family for long periods. What would they miss most?

3 The extract is really in two parts. Read down to the end of paragraph 2 first. How did Roald Dahl feel during this part of the journey? How well-prepared was he for what lay ahead? Were his parents right not to tell him much? *(He enjoyed the steamer trip but began to grow nervous when they landed. He was physically prepared but not mentally.)*

4 Discuss each of the things found in a tuck box. *(He had a magnet, a pocket-knife, a compass, a ball of string, a clockwork racing-car, lead soldiers, conjuring tricks, tiddly-winks, a jumping bean, a catapult, foreign stamps and stink-bombs.)* Discuss why they would be special to a nine-year-old boy.

5 Read the rest of the extract, from paragraph 2 onwards. Describe Roald's first impression of the school and the headmaster. *(The school*

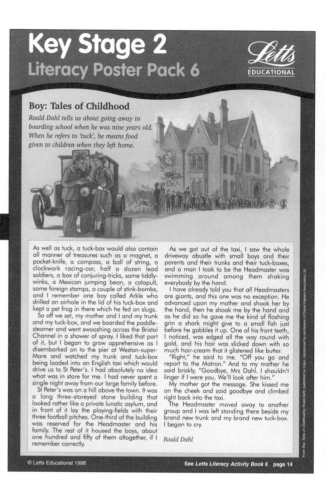

*looked like a lunatic asylum – grim and forbidding; the headmaster seemed tall and shark-like, or predatory.)* Why did Roald think he was a giant? *(Because of his physical size and his power over the boys.)* Was it cruel or kind of his mother to leave immediately? *(Answers will depend on the children's interpretation.)* Describe Roald's feelings at being left. *(He was upset and scared and began to cry.)*

### *Writing composition*

1 Encourage the children to retell the episode from the point of view of Roald's mother. How might she feel at leaving her son? What might she think of the school and headmaster?

2 Help the children to carry out some research on Roald Dahl. Ask them to write some biographical details about him. Remind them to keep the biography factual.

**3** Invite the children to discuss their very first memories of school. Ask them to write an autobiographical account of their first day, or something they remember vividly.

**4** Use the 'things found in a tuck box' idea as a stimulus for an alphabetical poem. Ask for suggestions along the 'things found on the school roof', 'things found in a school bag' line. Encourage the children to suggest ideas for things beginning with each letter of the alphabet. Compile a range of possibilities on the board. Refine the list and add appropriate phrases or descriptive words. Choose one item for each letter and compose a class list poem (it does not have to rhyme).

## SENTENCE Level
### Grammatical awareness

**1** Identify which of the sentences in the extract are written in the active form and which are written in the passive. *(There are many possible examples.)* Translate some of the active sentences into the passive form. *(The passive form is a sentence in which the subject is the person or thing acted upon by the verb, so 'The headmaster shook Roald's hand' – active. 'Roald's hand was shaken by the headmaster' – passive.)*

### Sentence construction and punctuation

**1** Look for connectives and conjunctions in the text which maintain cohesion and link phrases, clauses or sentences together. *(For example, 'So off we set', 'As we got out of the taxi… ', 'She kissed me on the cheek and… ', etc.)*

## WORD Level
### Spelling

**1** Look at the prefix in 'disembarked'. What effect does it have on the verb? *(It indicates reversal.)* Use dictionaries to find other words prefixed by 'dis-', 'im-', 'in-', or 'il-' which have a similar effect.

**2** Hold a 'syllable' hunt. Look for two- *(e.g. 'man/ner')*, three- *(e.g. 're/mem/ber')* and four-syllable *(e.g. 'al/to/ge/ther')* words in the text. *(There are many possible examples.)* Encourage the children to say the words and to mark syllable boundaries. As a class lesson, study the words and decide which are stressed and unstressed syllables. *(For example, 'man/ner'.)*

### Vocabulary extension

**1** The school Roald attended was named after a saint. Research the origins of the names of the days of the week and months of the year, and the names of products like models of cars, names of sportswear and names of newspapers, etc.

---

**Related texts:**

Other titles by Roald Dahl:
'James and the Giant Peach'

'Matilda'

About Roald Dahl:
'Roald Dahl' by John Malam

# The Wind in the Willows

## About the text

*This playscript extract is taken from an adaptation of the children's classic written by Kenneth Grahame.*

## Teaching opportunities at:

### TEXT Level

#### Reading comprehension

**1** Ask if any children have read the book or seen the film. Invite their comments and observations. What sort of character is Toad? Ask the children to suggest other books in which there are anthropomorphic characters (animals with human characteristics).

**2** Read the introduction and discuss how such introductions help the reader. *(They set the scene and put it in context.)*

**3** Ask the children to have a quick glance at the text and suggest what sort of a text it is. *(A playscript.)* Discuss some of the features that help the reader read it most effectively. *(The clear signposting of when different characters speak; the stage directions; the accompanying narrator's lines which link the dialogue together and set the scene, and the punctuation marks, of course!)*

**4** The extract can be divided into different sections: Toad with the rabbits; Toad with Badger, Rat and Mole; the episode with the car salesman; the last section (the right-hand column). Read each section to the class, one at a time.

**5** After the first section, ask the children to suggest where it is taking place. What can be learned about Mr Toad from the song? *(It takes place on the road and we learn that Mr Toad is rather fond of himself!)*

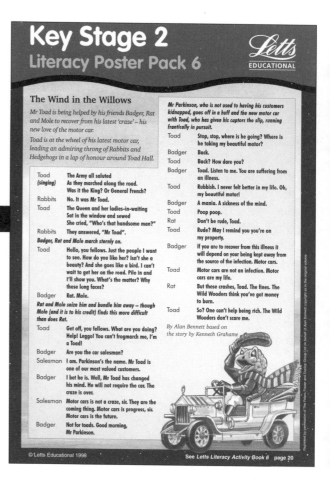

**Key Stage 2**
Literacy Poster Pack 6
*Letts* EDUCATIONAL

The Wind in the Willows

*Mr Toad is being helped by his friends Badger, Rat and Mole to recover from his latest 'craze' – his new love of the motor car.*

*Toad is at the wheel of his latest motor car, leading an admiring throng of Rabbits and Hedgehogs in a lap of honour around Toad Hall.*

**Toad** (singing) The Army all saluted / As they marched along the road. / Was it the King? Or General French?

**Rabbits** No. It was Mr Toad.

**Toad** The Queen and her ladies-in-waiting / Sat in the window and sewed / She cried, "Who's that handsome man?"

**Rabbits** They answered, "Mr Toad".

*Badger, Rat and Mole march sternly on.*

**Toad** Hello, you fellows. Just the people I want to see. How do you like her? Isn't she a beauty? And she goes like a bird. I can't wait to get her on the road. Pile in and I'll show you. What's the matter? Why these long faces?

**Badger** Rat. Mole.

*Rat and Mole seize him and bundle him away – though Mole (and it is to his credit) finds this more difficult than does Rat.*

**Toad** Get off, you fellows. What are you doing? Help! Leggo! You can't frogmarch me, I'm a Toad!

**Badger** Are you the car salesman?

**Salesman** I am. Parkinson's the name. Mr Toad is one of our most valued customers.

**Badger** I bet he is. Well, Mr Toad has changed his mind. He will not require the car. The craze is over.

**Salesman** Motor cars is not a craze, sir. They are the coming thing. Motor cars is progress, sir. Motor cars is the future.

**Badger** Not for toads. Good morning, Mr Parkinson.

*Mr Parkinson, who is not used to having his customers kidnapped, goes off in a huff and the new motor car with Toad, who has given his captors the slip, running frantically in pursuit.*

**Toad** Stop, stop, where is he going? Where is he taking my beautiful motor?

**Badger** Back.

**Toad** Back? How dare you?

**Badger** Toad. Listen to me. You are suffering from an illness.

**Toad** Rubbish. I never felt better in my life. Oh, my beautiful motor!

**Badger** A mania. A sickness of the mind.

**Toad** Poop poop.

**Rat** Don't be rude, Toad.

**Toad** Rude? May I remind you you're on my property.

**Badger** If you are to recover from this illness it will depend on your being kept away from the source of the infection. Motor cars.

**Toad** Motor cars are not an infection. Motor cars are my life.

**Rat** But these crashes, Toad. The fines. The Wild Wooders think you've got money to burn.

**Toad** So? One can't help being rich. The Wild Wooders don't scare me.

*By Alan Bennett based on the story by Kenneth Grahame*

© Letts Educational 1998                    See *Letts Literacy Activity Book 6*  page 20

**6** After the second section, discuss how Toad's attitude towards cars differs from that of Rat, Mole and Badger. *(Toad loves the car while the others think it is crazy and dangerous.)*

**7** After the third section, discuss what views the salesman holds about Toad and the cars. *(He thinks Toad is a valuable customer – he spends lots of money, and he thinks the car is 'progress' and 'the future'.)*

**8** After the last section, ask the children why Toad's friends consider his affection for cars 'an illness'? Do the children agree? Why or why not?

**9** Go back and look at the stage directions. How helpful would these be to the actors? *(They explain how the scene should run and provide the physical roles for each character.)*

**10** Encourage groups of children to practise and perform the play *(perhaps as a radio play with sound effects)*. Allow plenty of time for them to practise to get it right.

## Writing composition

**1** Discuss how the salesman would have perceived the whole affair. Encourage the children to retell the episode from his point of view, either in the first-person, or as a piece of continuous prose.

## SENTENCE Level
### Grammatical awareness

**1** Mr Parkinson, the salesman, says 'Motor cars is progress'. Notice that the noun and verb do not agree. Ask the children to write other things he might say, deliberately ensuring that the subjects and verbs do not agree in the sentences. Ask the children to think of expressions they have heard people use in which this happens, such as 'We was going', 'I done it' etc., then ask them to correct them into accurate, grammatical sentences.

**2** In Toad's last line he refers to himself as 'one'. Draw attention to this and discuss the use of this pronoun. *(The indefinite person, regarded as typical of every person.)* Point out that it is less and less commonly used and is considered rather formal.

### Sentence construction and punctuation

**1** There are many 'abbreviated' sentences in the play, such as 'Why these long faces' which often omit the verb. List some of these sentences. *(e.g. 'Or General French?', 'Not for toads', 'I never felt better in my life', 'Oh, my beautiful motor', 'But these crashes' and 'The fines'.)* Write their full meaning. *(For example, 'Was it General French?', 'Motor cars are not the future for toads', 'I have never felt better in my life', 'It is my beautiful motor', 'Think of these crashes' and 'Think of the fines'.)* Discuss the fact that a clause or sentence usually has a verb in it.

## WORD Level
### Spelling

**1** 'Craze' ends in '-aze'. Ask the children to think of some more '-aze' words or to look in other books. Ask them to suggest some '-ase' words, too. Extend this activity to include '-ize' and '-ise' words. *(Note '-ise' is now becoming far more common than '-ize', but some words may still be spelled with either ending.)*

**2** Find the 'ie' words in the text. *('Friends', 'ladies' and 'cried'.)* Do they follow the 'i before e' rule? *(Yes.)*

### Vocabulary extension

**1** There are three expressions containing references to animals in the text. Ask the children to try and find them. *('Frog-marched', 'kidnapped', 'she goes like a bird'.)* Ask them to suggest others they have read or to make up some of their own.

**2** Mr Toad refers to his car as 'she'. Use this as an opportunity to review work on gender, especially related to humans and animals. Discuss terms that are clearly gender-based and also that have become representative of both genders, e.g. cow/bull and hero.

**3** Find and list the compound words in the play. Can the children work out the words that make them up? *('Hedgehog', 'frogmarch' and 'salesman'.)* Ask the children to list some.

### Related texts:

Other titles by Kenneth Grahame:

'Mole's Christmas or Home Sweet Home'
'The Reluctant Dragon'
'The River Bank' adapted by Polly Whittacker

Classic stories in play form:

'Puss in Boots' by Moira Butterfield
'Children's Fairytale Theatre: Three Plays to Perform: Cinderella, Beauty and the Beast, Aladdin' by Terri Wiltshire

# I am David

## About the text

*This is an extract from the poignant book of the same name written by Anne Holm. It is about a 12-year-old boy who escapes from a prison camp during the Second World War.*

## Teaching opportunities at:

### TEXT Level
### Reading comprehension

**1** Before reading the text to the class, briefly set the scene by sketching in the context and any appropriate background information.

**2** Read the whole passage through once and encourage the children to articulate their responses to it in general, identifying why and how the text affected them. How successful has the author been in involving the reader with the main character and encouraging empathy? Did they like the way it was written?

**3** Ask the children to try to classify or describe this text in their own words, in fairly general terms.

**4** Explore the contrasts in the first paragraph. What does the first sentence mean? *(David has experienced much horror in a short life and can remember it all.)* Why would all the simple things he describes give him pleasure? *(Because they are associated with freedom.)* Discuss as a class how much we take for granted in our own everyday lives. Why is it taken for granted?

**5** What danger is David in? *(He is in danger of being discovered by the men.)* What clues are there? *(He is afraid of being heard and he can see the men waiting.)*

**Key Stage 2**
**Literacy Poster Pack 6**
*Letts EDUCATIONAL*

**I am David**

*It is the Second World War. David is 12 years old. He has spent years of his life in a prison camp, but has been given the chance to escape.*

David remembered all the pain and bitterness he had ever known – and how much he could remember in such a short time! He recalled, too, all the good things he had learned about since he had gained his freedom – beauty and laughter, music and kind people, Maria, and a tree smothered in pink blossom, a dog to walk by his side, and a place to aim for …

This would be the end. He pressed his face into the dog's long coat so that no one should hear him, and wept. He wept quite quietly, but the dog grew uneasy and wanted to whimper again.

David stopped crying. "God," he whispered, "God of the green pastures and still waters, I've one promise of help left, but it's too late now. You can't do anything about this. I don't mean to be rude, because I know you're very strong and you could make those men down there want to walk away for a bit. But they won't. They don't know, you see, and they're not afraid of you. But they are afraid of the commandant because he'll have them shot if they leave their posts. So you can see there's nothing you can do now. But please don't think I'm blaming you. It was my own fault for not seeing the danger in time. I shall run … Perhaps you'll see they aim straight so it doesn't hurt before I die. I'm so frightened of things that hurt. No, I forgot. I've only one promise of help left, and it's more important you should help the dog get away and find some good people to live with. Perhaps *they'll* shoot straight anyway, but if they don't it can't be helped: you must save the dog because it once tried to protect me. Thank you for having been my God: I'm glad I chose you. And now I must run, for if I leave it any longer I shan't have the courage to die. I am David. Amen."

The dog kept nudging him. It wanted them to go back the way they had come, away from the spot where it sensed danger lurking.

"No," David whispered, "we can't go back – it's too late. You must keep still, King; and when they've hit me, perhaps you can get away by yourself."

The dog licked his cheek eagerly, impatiently nudging him again and moving restlessly as if it wanted to get up. It nudged him once more – and then jumped up before David could stop it. In one swift second David understood what the dog wanted. It did not run back the way they had come. It was a sheepdog and it had sensed danger … It was going to take David's place! Barking loudly it sprang towards the men in the dark.

*Anne Holm*

© Letts Educational 1998

See *Letts Literacy Activity Book 6* page 22

**6** Ask the children what David's view of God is. Why doesn't David blame God for his situation? *(He blames himself for not seeing the danger.)* What request does David make of God? *(That He saves the dog.)* What does this tell the reader about David's character? *(He is generous and unselfish.)*

**7** Look for clues in the passage about the dog. Discuss its relationship with David, and its actions throughout the passage. *(It is a sheepdog called King and once saved David's life. It senses danger and helps once more by leaping ahead of David to distract the men.)*

**8** The author has written the novel from David's viewpoint. Would the children view David any differently if it had been written from the perspective of one of the soldiers?

## Writing composition

1 Encourage the children to make a quick plan of how the story might continue, in note form. Will any new characters become involved? Will David and the dog escape? Encourage the children to think creatively and not just go for the 'easy' option! Compare different ideas and encourage diversity. Ask the children to refine their ideas in the light of the discussion before attempting to write their story. Perhaps some could write it from a different viewpoint – perhaps as someone who witnesses the events intervenes and helps David.

## SENTENCE Level
### Grammatical awareness

1 Turn some of the sentences in the text into the passive form and discuss how word order and meaning are affected. *(For example, 'The dog licked David's cheek' would become 'David's cheek was licked by the dog'.)*

2 There are several abstract nouns in the passage such as 'courage'. Find some more and ask the children to suggest others. *('Pain', 'bitterness', 'beauty', 'laughter', 'fault' and 'danger').*

### Sentence construction and punctuation

1 Read the last part of the story again, from 'The dog kept nudging him'. Explore how the sequence of events is connected together and structured by significant words and phrases.

2 Select some complex sentences from the text and identify the clauses from which they are made. In each sentence is there a main clause? *(Answers will depend on the sentences chosen.)*

## WORD Level
### Spelling

1 Ask the children to find some words in the text which have been suffixed or prefixed in some way. *(There are many possible examples.)* Identify and write the root word in each, noting if and how its spelling has been altered. Consider the effect of the suffix or prefix on each word, too.

### Vocabulary extension

1 Search for words in the text that could be spelled a different way, yet still sound the same (homonyms). *('Pain/pane', 'time/thyme', 'too/too/to', 'by/buy', 'place/plaice', 'for/four', 'would/wood', 'be/bee', 'so/sew', 'one/won', 'hear/here', 'no/know', 'there/their', 'see/sea', 'straight/strait', 'die/dye', 'way/weight', 'more/ moor' and 'not/knot'.)* Ask the children to compose pairs of sentences, using the words to show they understand their meanings.

### Related texts:

Other titles by Anne Holm:

'The Hostage'
'The Sky Grew Red'

Other titles about the Second World War:

'Goodnight Mr Tom' by Michelle Magorian
'Back Home' by Michelle Magorian
'Going Back' by Penelope Lively
'The Endless Steppe' by Esther Hautzig
'The Diary of Anne Frank' by Anne Frank

# The Secret Diary of Adrian Mole Aged Thirteen and Three Quarters

## *About the text*

*This poster is based on three days from the diary of Adrian Mole (aged thirteen and three quarters). All the angst of adolescence is captured by Sue Townsend as Adrian records everyday events and his thoughts and feelings.*

## Teaching opportunities at:

### TEXT Level
### *Reading comprehension*

**1** Read the title and look at the illustration. Ask the children to glance briefly at the text and who wrote it. What sort of text is it going to be? *(A diary.)* How can you tell? *(The layout is paragraphed into dates.)* What does 'when the extra three quarters can make all the difference' in the introduction mean? *(It means that at that age, every second of life is important, whereas they become less so as one grows older.)* Is the diary intended to be serious or not? What impression does the picture give? *(It is not serious as the comic-style illustration indicates.)* Is Adrian Mole a real person? Did he write the diary? *(It is fiction written by Sue Townsend.)*

**2** Read the diary one day at a time. What is the first day's entry mainly about? *(A picture Adrian painted in Art.)* What can be inferred about Nigel from it? *(Answers will depend on the children's interpretation, but one inference is that Nigel has 'stolen' Adrian's girlfriend.)* The last sentence, 'Ms Fossington-Gore said my picture "had depth", so did the river' is a play on words, with a double meaning. Ask the children to explain it.

**3** Read Wednesday's entry. Ask the children to work out the meaning of the term 'namby-pamby'. *(To take too good care of or molly-coddle.)* Explain how Adrian uses his diary to express his feeling that life is unfair at times and that his mother doesn't understand him. How does he feel he pays her back? *(The mud from his dirty clothes clogs up her washing machine.)* What might the last entry of the day mean? *(It refers to his lost girlfriend.)*

**4** Read the last day's entry. How does Adrian feel about the dog? Why might it have been at the vets? Why does he say 'This means the dog will soon starve'? *(Answers will depend on the children's interpretation.)*

**5** This diary has similar features to most diaries. Discuss that fact that it is written in the past tense; that it is in the first-person; that it is written at different times; why there are so many personal details; why it sounds like a conversation.

## Writing composition

1 In the diary we get a reasonable picture of the sort of person Adrian is. We also get a glimpse of his mother and father from Adrian's point of view. Ask the children to imagine his mother or father kept a diary. How would they have described Adrian? What sort of things would they have written about? Brainstorm ideas and encourage the children to write an imaginary diary for the same period, from the point of view of the mother or father. Remind them of the features of a typical diary as previously discussed.

## SENTENCE Level
### Grammatical awareness

1 Write several sentences in the passive, adapted from and based on entries in the diary, such as 'Adrian was told by his teacher that his picture had "depth",' and 'The picture was painted by Adrian'. Ask the children to rewrite these in the active form and discuss how the wording and sense of the sentences changes.

### Sentence construction and punctuation

1 Study the use of punctuation and italics in the diary and how they provide emphasis. Discuss the function each type of punctuation has, and how each helps the reader. Using other reading books, explore the role played by more sophisticated punctuation marks like colons, semi-colons, parenthetic commas, dashes and brackets.

## WORD Level
### Spelling

1 Explore the use of double consonants at the end and in the middle of words. Why are double consonants needed – why is it not possible to use single consonants in these situations? *(The double consonant ensures the vowel retains its short sound, e.g. 'hoping', 'hopping'.)* Ask the children to suggest other words that fit the pattern of these words.

2 Note the sound of 'ch' in 'machine' and 'school'. Ask the children to think of other 'ch' words for both the hard and soft pronunciation. Look at the word 'torrential'. Which letters make the 'sh' sound in it? Think of and list other words ending in '-tial'. *(There are many possible examples.)*

### Vocabulary extension

1 Adrian describes Art as 'dead good'. Ask the children to suggest other common expressions for something good, e.g. 'brilliant', 'super', etc. These expressions often change over time. Ask the children to find words expressions for 'good' that are now no longer popular. Suggest some of the war-time expressions, like 'spiffing' or 'jolly'. Books about Biggles and Just William should be a useful source.

2 Carry out the same exercise for words and expressions which mean 'not good', like 'rubbish', 'ballyhoo', 'bosh', 'guff', 'ripe', 'balderdash', tommyrot', etc.

---

### Related texts:

Other titles by Sue Townsend:
'The Growing Pains of Adrian Mole'

Other diary titles:
'The Diary of Anne Frank' by Anne Frank
'Strider' by Beverly Clearly

# Anne Frank Beyond the Diary

## About the text

*This extract is taken from the biography of Anne Frank, whose diary tells of her family's experiences when hiding from the Nazis in Amsterdam during the Second World War.*

**Key Stage 2**
Literacy Poster Pack 6
*Letts*
EDUCATIONAL

**Anne Frank Beyond the Diary**

*This extract is taken from the biography of Anne Frank, whose diary tells of her family's experiences when hiding from the Nazis in Amsterdam during the Second World War.*

What did Anne do during those long daytime hours? She spent a lot of time studying her schoolbooks, a large pile of which had been taken along. She also read many books which Miep brought her, and learned shorthand. Margot and Peter also spent many hours on their schoolwork every day. Otto Frank helped all three children and tested them on their lessons. None of them wanted to fall behind in their studies. They still hoped that they would be able to return to school soon.

Many Jews in the Netherlands were picked up during these months and taken to concentration camps. Though the Frank and Van Pels families had escaped this, they could not escape being crowded on top of each other day and night. They saw and heard everything everyone did. This lack of privacy, as well as the never-ending fear of discovery, put everyone constantly on edge. It is therefore not surprising that arguments were a regular part of life in the Annex.

Anne wrote: *Why do grownups quarrel so easily, so much, and over the most idiotic things? Up till now I thought that only children squabbled.* (September 28, 1942)

Anne, too, found her new life difficult. She had lost everything: her friends, her school, her freedom. Sometimes she rebelled, and sometimes sadness overtook her and she often cried at night. But during the day she was different: lively and boisterous, and usually surprisingly cheerful. She had something to say about everything and everyone, and was always ready with a quick answer. Mr and Mrs Van Pels thought her behaviour insolent and believed she had been brought up badly. Edith Frank regularly argued with Anne, and Margot was often short-tempered with her. Peter wasn't much help, either.

*Margot and Peter aren't a bit what you would call 'young', they are both so staid and quiet. I show up terribly against them and am always hearing "You don't find Margot and Peter doing that – why don't you just once follow your dear sister's example?" I simply loathe it.* (February 5, 1943)

Anne felt truly alone and misunderstood. Her diary had become her one really good friend.

Most of the time life in the Annex was simply boring. Yet there were also moments of great excitement – and great fear. One evening at eight o'clock the bell suddenly rang loudly. Everyone was terrified. Was it the German police, the Gestapo? Was it the end? They all held their breaths. But there was no more noise.

*Ruud van der Rol and Rian Verhoeven*

© Letts Educational 1998

See *Letts Literacy Activity Book 6* page 26

# Teaching opportunities at:

## TEXT Level
### Reading comprehension

**1** Read the text to the class. Sketch in the background briefly, as appropriate, to set the passage in context. Discuss with the class some of the pressures, difficulties, trials and tribulations, and fears of living in such conditions. What sort of things would they take with them into hiding? What would they miss most? What wouldn't they be able to do?

**2** The passage talks about 'life in the Annex'. What picture do the children have in their mind of the 'Annex'?

**3** List the characters mentioned. *(Anne Frank, Miep, Margot, Peter, Otto Frank, Mr and Mrs Van Pels and Edith Frank.)* Ask the children to piece together their relationships. *(The only clear relationships are that Margot and Peter are brother and sister to Anne, though it is likely from the text that Edith Frank is their mother and the Van Pels are family friends.)*

**4** Ask the children what sort of things Anne did all day. *(She studied her schoolbooks, read and learned shorthand.)*

**5** Why was there so much arguing in the Annex. Is this surprising? *(This will depend on the children's interpretation.)*

**6** Describe the contrasts in Anne's behaviour in paragraph 4. How do the children think these can be explained?

**7** Ask the children to explain why Anne's diary 'became her best friend'.

**8** This passage provides a good opportunity to investigate the differences between biographical and autobiographical writing as it contains examples of both. Identify and list some of the differences. *(Biographical: written in past tense, third-person, mainly factual, more formal style; autobiographical: present tense, first-person, personal details and thoughts, conversational style.)*

## Writing composition

**1** Ask the children to write a description of a friend, or someone they admire, perhaps a famous footballer or musician, as a piece of biographical writing. Discuss with the class the sort of things that could be included and how the text could be structured.

**2** Discuss and show the children an example of a CV. Explain why and how they are used. Note the way they are set out and the sort of information included. Ask them to write one for themselves.

# SENTENCE Level
## Grammatical awareness

**1** Use the text as a basis for reviewing work on word classes. Select one particular class of word at a time, for example, nouns. Read through the passage and identify all the nouns. Ask the children to say whether they are singular or plural, common, proper, abstract or collective, etc. Apply the same sort of approach to other classes of words, such as verbs, adjectives, adverbs, pronouns, prepositions, etc. *(There are many possible examples for all the above.)*

## Sentence construction and punctuation

**1** Explore the use of connectives and conjunctions in the text which maintain cohesion in the text and link phrases, clauses or sentences together. *(There are many possible examples.)* In paragraph 2, note the use of words like 'though', 'as well as' and 'therefore' which help structure it.

**2** Select some complex sentences from the text and identify the clauses from which they are made. In each sentence is there a main clause? *(There are many possible examples.)*

# WORD Level
## Spelling

**1** Find and list some words containing the vowel 'o' only once. *(For example, 'from', 'of', 'world', 'do', 'long', 'lot', 'shorthand', 'none', 'work', 'once', etc.)* Try to categorise the words according to the way the 'o' is pronounced. Do any patterns emerge?

**2** Carry out investigations of this type for the other vowels and ask the children to list the vowels and their sounds in a table. Note that many words 'borrowed' from other languages (especially Italian) end in 'a', 'o' or 'i', for example, 'opera', 'concerto' and 'spaghetti'.

## Vocabulary extension

**1** People from Holland are called 'Dutch'. List some other countries and how their people are described.

**2** Our language is full of words we have 'borrowed' from other languages. The Dutch were great traders in the 17th century. We have borrowed many words to do with ships from them, such as 'yacht', 'smuggle', 'skipper', 'schooner' and 'reef'. Check the etymology of these words in an etymological dictionary, if possible. Here are some others for children to check, too: from Italy come 'pizza', 'balcony', 'opera', 'piano'; from France come 'banquet', 'biscuit'; from India come 'bungalow', 'verandah', 'jungle'; and from the Middle East come 'bazaar', 'caravan', 'turban'.

### Related texts:

More information books on Anne Frank:

'Anne Frank' by Harriet Castor and David Adler
'Anne Frank' by Wayne Jackman

Second World War books:

'World War 2' by Neil Thomson
('When I was young' type of narrative)
'Overlord' by Christopher Hudson
(personal narrative)
'I am David' by Anne Holm

# Penny for the Guy

## About the text

*Henry Mayhew was a Victorian journalist who wrote about the lives of the poor. This passage is about what poor Victorian children did on November 5th.*

## Teaching opportunities at:

### TEXT Level
### Reading comprehension

**1** Read the title and introduction, and look at the illustrations. Before reading the passage, ask the children what they do on November 5th. Ask them to share their knowledge about the history of November 5th and why and how it is celebrated today. Explain that for some of the poor children in Victorian times, it was also a way of making money.

**2** The text can be divided into three sections – the making of the guy (the first column), taking the guy round 'Holborn way' (most of the second column) and the episode with the other gang (beginning 'At last… ').

**3** First of all, read the whole passage through. Ask the children how it could be written in three paragraphs. *(It isn't set out this way because when we speak, it is a continuous flow! Punctuation marks are a written convention.)*

**4** Read the first section, reminding the children that the text is a record of what the child actually said. How can you tell this? *(It is written in the first-person.)* How well does the child describe the process of being made up? *(It is quite detailed, yet rambling, but it is easy to picture.)* Ask the children to list the steps in the process. *(Drape paper-hangings round the legs – put on an apron – dress it with tinsel bows – a tail – a tinsel heart and rosettes in green and red – prepare a black mask with red on the cheeks, like a devil, and with horns.)*

**Key Stage 2**
**Literacy Poster Pack 6**
*Letts EDUCATIONAL*

**Penny for the Guy**

*Henry Mayhew was a journalist in the 1850s. He was one of the first people to write about the poor in London. Here he interviews some boys about what they did on 5 November.*

I couldn't have been more than seven years old when I first began. They put paper-hangings round my legs – sometimes they bought, and sometimes they got it given to them; but they gave a rare lot for a penny or twopence. After that they put on me an apron made of the same sort of paper – showy, you know, then they put a lot of tinsel bows, and at the corners they cut a sort of tail … it looked stunnin'; then they put on my chest a tinsel heart and rosettes; they were green and red because it shows off. All up my arms I had bows and things to make a showoff. Then I put on a black mask with a little red on the cheek, to make me look like a devil: it had horns, too. Why, he made me a little guy about a foot high, to carry in my lap. It was made to sit in a chair; and there was a piece of string tied to each of the legs and the arms; and a string came behind; and I used to pull it, and the legs and arms jumped up.

I was put in a chair, and two old broom-handles were put through the rails, and then a boy got in front, and another behind; and carried me off round Holborn way in the streets and squares. Every now and then they put me down before a window; then one of 'em used to say the speech, and I used all the time to keep pulling the string of my little guy, and it amused the children – them of them went and knocked at the door and asked "Please to remember the Guy"; and the little children brought us ha'pence and pence; sometimes the ladies and gentlemen chucked money out of the window. At last they carried me into Russell Square. They put me down before a gentleman's house and began saying the speech: while they were saying it, up comes a lot of boys with sticks in their hands.

After a bit one of these boys says "Oh, it's a dead guy; let's have a lark with it!" and then one of 'em gives me a punch in the eye with his fist and then snatched the mask off my face, and when he pulled it off he says, "Oh, Bill, it's a live 'un!" We were afraid that we should get the worst of it, so we ran way round the Square. After we'd run a little way they caught us up again and says, "Now then, give us all your money." With that, some ladies and gentlemen that saw it all came up and says, "If you don't go, we'll lock you up"; and so they let us go away. And so we went to another place where they sold masks and we bought another.

*Henry Mayhew*

© Letts Educational 1998        See *Letts Literacy Activity Book 6*   page 28

**5** Read the second section. Ask the children to describe the technique of the group for gaining attention and getting money. *(They would say a speech and the guy would make the puppet dance; they would also knock on doors.)* Was this the same as begging? *(Not quite, as the children are doing something for the money.)*

**6** Read the third section. Were the second group of boys bullies or were they just trying to survive like the others? *(Answers depend on the children's interpretation, though they are primarily bullies.)* We often use the expression 'All's well that ends well'. Discuss how this might describe the outcome of the episode.

**7** Was the child more than seven when he was interviewed? How can you tell? *(Yes, because it is a reminiscence.)* Why was the passage written in the past tense? *(It is a memory of events from the past.)*

**8** Does the child speak in 'standard English'? *(No.)* Find and discuss examples of the use of non-standard English. *(There are many possible examples.)*

## Writing composition

**1** Ask the children to make up some imaginary interviews with historical or contemporary characters and report them verbatim, in the style of the passage. Discuss who they might choose, what sort of things the characters might say and how they might say them. If historical characters are chosen, discuss how important some preliminary research might be for authenticity's sake.

**2** Children could carry out interviews with relatives, or members of the school staff, asking them to recount vivid childhood memories. This could be recorded and transcribed in the style of the passage. Alternatively, you could recount an early childhood memory to them, and ask them to write up their version of what you said. Compare the results and discuss the different versions.

## SENTENCE Level
### Grammatical awareness

**1** Ask the children to rewrite sections of the passage, rewording and clarifying unclear parts, rephrasing expressions and sections in more conventional standard English.

## Sentence construction and punctuation

**1** The interview consists of a lot of clauses strung together, using the conjunction 'and' to join them. Take a small section and restructure it, omitting the over-use of 'and'.

## WORD Level
### Spelling

**1** Find some words in the text that make the sound 'air'. *(For example, 'chair', 'rare' and 'their'.)* Ask the children to supply some other words with these letter patterns and sounds, both from the text and from other books.

**2** Hold other 'letter pattern' hunts based on the text. Supply patterns for children to look for, such as 'el', 'ear', 'gh', etc. *(For example, 'tins<u>el</u>', 'y<u>ear</u>', 'bou<u>gh</u>t', etc.)* Build up word lists based on these for spelling practice.

### Vocabulary extension

**1** The passage is full of words or expressions used in Victorian times. List some of these *(for example, 'let's have a lark with it')*, and ask the children to write them as we might say them today.

**2** There are many examples of apostrophes used to denote missing letters. Write these in full. *('Couldn't/could not', 'stunnin/stunning', ''em/them', 'ha'pence/halfpence', 'it's/it is', ''un/one' and 'we'll/we will'.)*

---

### Related texts:

Information books on Guy Fawkes:
'Guy Fawkes' by Clare Chandler
'The Gunpowder Plot' by Rhoda Nottridge

Information books on Victorian England:
'Victorian Children' by Jane Shuter
'How We Used to Live: Victorians Early and Late' by David Evans

# The Iron Man

## *About the text*

*This extract is from the Ted Hughes children's classic of the same name.*

### Key Stage 2
Literacy Poster Pack 6 — *Letts* EDUCATIONAL

#### The Iron Man

*The Iron Man has appeared in the countryside and is causing havoc, eating everything metal he can find. The local farmers have to think of a way to stop him.*

The Iron Man stood up straight. Slowly he turned, till he was looking directly at Hogarth.

"We're sorry we trapped you and buried you," shouted the little boy. "We promise we'll not deceive you again. Follow us and you can have all the metal you want. Brass too. Aluminium too. And lots of old chrome. Follow us."

The Iron Man pushed aside the boughs and came into the lane, Hogarth joined the farmers. Slowly they drove back down the lane, and slowly, with all his cogs humming, the Iron Man stepped after them.

They led through the villages. Half the people came out to stare, half ran to shut themselves inside bedrooms and kitchens. Nobody could believe their eyes when they saw the Iron Man marching behind the farmers.

At last they came to the town, and there was a great scrap-metal yard. Everything was there, old cars by the hundred, old trucks, old railway engines, old stoves, old refrigerators, old springs, bedsteads, bicycles, girders, gates, pans – all the scrap iron of the region was piled up there, rusting away.

"There," cried Hogarth.
"Eat all you can."

The Iron Man gazed, and his eyes turned red. He kneeled down in the yard, he stretched out on one elbow. He picked up a greasy black stove and chewed on it. He followed that with a double-decker bedstead and the brass knobs made his eyes crackle with joy. Never before had the Iron Man eaten such delicacies. As he lay there, a big truck turned into the yard and unloaded a pile of rusty chain. The Iron Man lifted a handful and let it dangle into his mouth – better than any spaghetti.

So there they left him. It was an Iron Man's heaven. The farmers went back to their farms. Hogarth visited the Iron Man every few days. Now the Iron Man's eyes were constantly a happy blue. He was no longer rusty. His body gleamed blue, like a new gun barrel. And he ate, ate, ate, ate – endlessly.

*Ted Hughes*

© Letts Educational 1998

See *Letts Literacy Activity Book 6* page 34

## Teaching opportunities at:

### TEXT Level
### *Reading comprehension*

**1** Before reading the passage, ask if any of the children have read the book. If any have, ask them to recount what they can remember of it, to help set the context for the extract.

**2** Read the passage to and with the class and ask the children for their immediate reactions to the text. Did they like it? Encourage them to articulate their thoughts and opinions.

**3** Who is Hogarth? *(Hogarth is a little boy – the hero.)* How old is he? *(Answers will depend on the children's interpretation.)* Could he be described as 'brave'? *(Answers will depend on the children's interpretation, but his actions could be described as brave.)*

**4** What had happened in the book before this episode? *(The Iron Man had appeared and begun to eat everything metal he could find.)*

**5** Describe and explain the Iron Man's reaction when he saw the scrap-metal yard. *(His eyes turn red and 'crackle with joy'.)*

**6** Why is the scrap yard described as 'the Iron Man's heaven'? *(It is filled with everything metal, and metal is all he eats.)*

**7** What was the Iron Man's body like at the beginning of the passage? What was it like at the end? How can this be explained? *(It was rusty and stiff but when he began to eat, it became smooth and shiny – the result of a 'good' diet for him.)*

**8** How does the writer manage to capture a feeling of menace at the beginning and tranquillity at the end of the extract? *(The menace comes from the Iron Man seeming unstoppable and huge, destroying things in his path. By the end, he is happy and healthy, and no longer frightening.)*

**9** How would children describe this type of writing? Do they think it is adventure, sci-fi, an animal story, etc.?

## Writing composition

1 The extract comes from the middle of the book. Ask the children to think about what might have happened at the beginning of the book, or what might happen next. Brainstorm ideas in note form under the two headings. Consider what characters might be involved, where the events might happen and any ideas for the plot. Allow the children to use these ideas as a basis for stimulating their own story. After the children write a first draft, discuss them, considering the language used, the layout, any paragraphing, use of dialogue, accuracy of spelling, etc. Then encourage them to write up a finished version, taking into account the comments of others.

## SENTENCE Level
### Grammatical awareness

1 Write some sentences on the board based on the text for the children to rewrite in the passive. (*For instance, 'The Iron Man looked at Hogarth' becomes 'Hogarth was looked at by the Iron Man'.*) Analyse the difference in word order, meaning, etc., and discuss any impact it has on the power of the passage.

### Sentence construction and punctuation

1 Explore the use of connectives and conjunctions in the text which maintain cohesion in the text and link phrases, clauses or sentences together, such as, 'Never before had the Iron Man eaten such delicacies' and 'As he lay there… '.

2 Provide the children with a list of common conjunctions (*for example, 'and', 'but', 'because', 'however', 'until', so, etc.*), and ask them to make up sentences containing them. How many clauses does each sentence have?

## WORD Level
### Spelling

1 Find the examples of 'ie' words in the text. (*'Buried', 'believe', 'cried' and 'delicacies'.*) Study them to see if they stick to the 'i before e except after c' rule. (*All but 'delicacies' do but this one breaks the rule.*) Ask the children to suggest a given number of other 'ie' words, perhaps by looking in other books.

2 Of the 'ie' words in the text, ask which are plurals of consonant plus 'y' words, and which are the past tenses. (*'Delicacies' – 'delicacy'; 'buried' – 'bury'; 'cried' – 'cry'.*) Ask the children to supply a given number of other words, say ten, for each category.

### Vocabulary extension

1 'Spaghetti' is a word we have 'borrowed' from Italian. Use an etymological dictionary to find where these other food words derive from. (*For instance, 'bread' is from the old English; 'cake' is from Viking; 'sausage' is from France; 'sugar' is from the Middle East; 'candy' is from America; 'pasta' is from Italy; 'kebab' is from India; and 'wok' is from China.*)

### Related texts:

Other titles by Ted Hughes:
'The Coming of the Kings and other Plays'
'The Dreamfighter and Other Creation Stories'
'The Earth-Owl and Other Moon People'
'Ffangs the Vampire Bat and the Kiss of Truth'
'How the Whale Became'
'The Iron Woman'
'Meet My Folks'
'Moon – Whales'
'Nessie the Mannerless Monster'

# Colonel Fazackerley

## About the text

*Colonel Fazackerley lives in a haunted house, but this humorous poem shows that he is not put off by the ghost at all!*

# Teaching opportunities at:

## TEXT Level
### Reading comprehension

**1** Read the poem to and with the class. After the first reading, ask the children to respond in general terms. What did they think of it? What did they like or not like about it? What struck them most about the poem?

**2** Ghosts are often portrayed as frightening characters. Make a list of the sort of things children think of when they imagine ghosts. Look at the various characteristics the ghost has in the poem. Look at the way the ghost is described. How well does it fit the stereotypical view of ghosts? *(The ghost does all the actions that would be expected of it, so it does fit.)*

**3** Discuss how this poem uses parody to undermine the stock character-type. *(Parody is a literary caricature which emphasises particular aspects of language or form to humorous effect, in this case by the unflustered responses of Colonel Fazackerley, which are not the usual stock-literary response to ghosts.)*

**4** Do the children think that the Colonel realises it is really a ghost, or does he think it is someone dressed up? *(Comparison of verse three with the last verse will show that, although he suggests initially that it is someone dressed up, he doesn't really think so.)*

**5** Find and discuss the effectiveness of some of the powerfully descriptive words used in the poem, e.g. 'clattered', 'shivered', etc. What do they bring to the poem and how do they affect how it is read?

**6** Discuss how the poem is structured. *(Include the verses, the lines per verse, rhyming couplets, etc.)*

**7** How can you tell the Colonel lived some years ago? *(By his description as wearing a 'monocle', by the way he spoke and by his appearance in the picture.)*

## Writing composition

**1** List a range of character-types on the board, such as trolls, giants, dragons, monsters, witches, lions, princesses, headteachers, etc. Ask the children to suggest characteristics that come to mind about each, and write them down under the particular character. Encourage the development of character stereotypes. Then ask the children to think of storylines in which the characters act 'out of character' or in the opposite way to that normally expected.

**2** This kind of thinking could also be applied to familiar traditional stories like 'Little Red Riding Hood' in which the characters can be made to act contrary to their usual roles.

## SENTENCE Level
### Grammatical awareness

**1** Draw attention to the way the poem has played around with word order as with 'Said the Colonel, "With laughter I'm feeling quite weak"'. Ask the children to rewrite selected sentences, using more conventional word order. Does it lessen the impact of the poem?

### Sentence construction and punctuation

**1** Ask the children to identify the use of connectives and conjunctions in the text which link phrases, clauses or sentences together, so 'On the very first evening', 'When the ghost', 'At this', etc.

## WORD Level
### Spelling

**1** Ask the children to volunteer some tricky words from the poem, such as 'castle', 'phosphorous', 'chimney', etc. Ask them for suggestions on how they could remember them. (*Suggest underlining the difficult parts; saying the words as they are written; making up silly sentences or mnemonics; looking for smaller, known words inside each longer word; using the 'Look, say, cover, write, check' method.*)

### Vocabulary extension

**1** What do the children think the Colonel means by the phrases 'That's really first class' and 'Give us a turn'? (*'A fine performance' and 'putting on a show'.*)

**2** Ask the children to volunteer things adults say that might sometimes puzzle them like 'Pull your socks up' or 'It's raining cats and dogs.' Discuss what these mean and how they might have arisen.

### Related texts:

Other works by Charles Causley:

'The Animals' Carol'
'Bring in the Holly'
'Early in the Morning: A Collection of New Poems'
'Figgie Hobbin'

Other 'spooky' poems:

'Creepy Poems' – Usborne Publishers
'Spooky Poems' – Mammouth Publishers

Ghost stories:

'Mr Corbett's Ghost and Other Stories' by Leon Garfield
'Moondial' by Helen Cresswell
'The Ghost at No. 13' by Giles Brandreth
'A Bad Case of Ghosts' by Kenneth Oppel
'Puffin Book of Ghosts and Ghouls' edited by Gene Kemp
'The Ghost Downstairs' by Leon Garfield

# The Sword in the Stone

## *About the text*

*In this extract from the book by T. H. White, two wizards have a competition to see who is smartest – in which tactics count for everything.*

© Letts Educational 1998      See *Letts Literacy Activity Book 6*   page 38

## Teaching opportunities at:

### TEXT Level
### *Reading comprehension*

**1** Read the passage to and with the class. Who are the two main 'combatants' in the competition? *(They are Merlyn and Madame Mim.)* What are they? *(Merlyn is a magician and Madame Mim is a witch.)* What special skills do they possess? *(They have magic powers and can transform themselves into anything they choose.)* In what way is the competition written about as if it were a boxing or a wrestling match? *(It is enacted in 'rounds' signalled by a gong and they have 'seconds' to assist them.)*

**2** Is the competition a bit of fun or is it more serious than that? What evidence is there of this? *(It is very serious as they both want to win – they are 'two desperate wizards'.)*

**3** In what way does Merlyn surprise Madame Mim? *(He copies the creatures she turns into.)* How does he 'break the rules'? *(He doesn't follow Madame Mim's opening gambit in the usual fashion.)* Are these rules written down or just accepted as the 'usual way' of doing things? *(Just accepted as far as we know.)* Is Merlyn cheating, or just being clever? *(He is being clever and following a plan.)*

**4** What effect do Merlyn's unusual tactics have on Madame Mim? *(They make her angry and disconcert her.)*

**5** Who is watching the competition? *(Hecate, who holds the coats; Wart, who speaks; and Archimedes, who 'gave Merlyn a little massage'.)* How can you tell Wart is watching with great interest? *(He holds his breath.)* What is Archimedes? How can you tell? *(He is a bird as he nibbles Merlyn with his beak.)*

**6** Analyse how the text is structured. Why has the writer divided it into paragraphs? *(For clarity and sense.)* Ask the children to list the main point of each paragraph. *(Merlyn and Madame Mim get ready for battle – they begin to fight – Merlyn copies Madame Mim's moves – Madame Mim changes tactics – the end of round one – the second round begins.)*

**7** How does the writer signal the passing of time? Discuss terms like 'become next', 'took her more than a minute', 'at this moment', etc., and how they keep the story moving.

## Writing composition

1 Discuss the idea of flashbacks as a literary device as a way of conveying the passing of time with the children. Use the passage as a springboard for experimenting with the device. Consider what might have led up to this episode. What might the two be trying to prove? Suggest that the children continue the story with a flashback. Give the opening line to them and ask them to continue the story. *(For example, 'As Merlyn stood facing Madame Mim, his mind flashed back to the events that led up to this silly trial of strength… ')* Compare and discuss different versions. Can they be improved in the light of everyone's comments?

## SENTENCE Level
### Grammatical awareness

1 Ensure that the children know the difference between the active and passive voice. In the active voice, the writer uses active verbs to make clear who carries out particular actions, so 'Hecate wore an eye-shade'. In the passive voice, this would be written 'An eye-shade was worn by Hecate'. Find some examples of active and passive voices being used in the text. *(There are many possible examples.)* Then ask the children to try to transform some of the active forms into the passive.

### Sentence construction and punctuation

1 Choose some sentences from the text and ask the children to try rewriting them in different ways while maintaining the same meaning. *(So 'Wart held his breath to see what the mouse would become next' could become 'With his breath held, Wart waited to see what the mouse would next become'.)*

## WORD Level
### Spelling

1 Use the words 'preliminary', 'invisible', 'irregular', 'unusual', 'internal' and 'surcoats' to focus on the use of prefixes and the way they change the meaning of words. Use the dictionary to find more words with these prefixes. Extend this to further work on prefixes such as 'sub-', 'bi-', 'tri-', 'con-' and 'ex-'.

### Vocabulary extension

1 Madame Mim and Merlyn are called wizards in the text. As Madame is a female term, should she be called a wizard or a witch? Discuss the differences, if any, in meaning. Use this as a means to discuss other gender issues like other names that are clearly male or female gender-specific. *('Man/woman', 'husband/wife', 'cow/bull', 'mare/stallion'.)* Introduce the idea of neuter *(without gender, as in 'table')* and common *(where it is impossible to tell the gender, as in 'children', 'teacher', 'pupil')*. Some words may now be applied to both males and females. *(For example, 'actor' and 'hero' are often used for both even though both have a feminine version.)* Look in books and find examples of the latter two types.

### Related texts:

Other 'Arthurian' stories:

'Mightier than the Sword' by Clare Bevan (a modern story about a boy who gets so involved in the stories he has heard about King Arthur that he decides he needs a cause to fight for)

'King Arthur and His Knights of the Round Table' by Roger Lancelyn Green

Modern witch stories:

'The Witches' by Roald Dahl

## Facts on Alcohol

### About the text

*This is a fairly typical example of a factual leaflet, detailing the relationship between drinking and driving, and the effects of alcohol.*

## Teaching opportunities at:

### TEXT Level
### Reading comprehension

**1** Look at the leaflet as a whole, at the illustration, and the sub-headings. Ask the children what the theme of the text is going to be. *(How alcohol affects performance, how it is measured and what might be a result of drinking.)* Ask them to volunteer any knowledge they may have on the subject and to raise questions they would like to see answered in the text. *(You may need to handle this issue with sensitivity.)*

**2** Ask the children where they might find specific information by scanning very briefly, for instance, where would they find how a breathalyser works? Ask them under which heading they would look.

**3** Close-read the text to and with the class, all the way through. Follow this by specific questions related to the factual content of the text, requiring them to scan for the specific answers, like 'What does "over the limit" mean?'

**4** Focus on one or two sections. Go through and discuss which are the facts and which are opinions, and make two lists.

**5** Find sentences or words used that make drinkers appear foolish, or anti-social, and which put drinking and driving in a negative light. *(For example, 'stupid', 'selfishly', 'no excuse', 'little sympathy', etc.)* What statistical evidence is provided in the text? *(See the box at the bottom of the poster.)*

**6** Ask the children for their opinion on the presentation, structure and layout of the article. How easy did they find making their way around? What 'signposts' are there to help the reader? *(Paragraphs, box text and sub-headings.)*

### Writing composition

**1** Encourage the children to write an argument in favour of something they feel strongly about, such as the value of pets, not having homework, working for pocket money, etc. Provide them with a structured framework to help them retain a shape to their argument.

*For example:*
*Framework 1: 'I think that... because...*
*I believe this because, firstly... so... Another reason is... because... I believe that my ideas show that... '*

*Framework 2: 'I would like to suggest that...
My reasons for believing this are...
Furthermore... Therefore, although some people
might argue... I believe my case is stronger and
have shown that... '*

## SENTENCE Level
### Grammatical awareness

1 Discuss why such leaflets are produced. Who
are they aimed at? Focus on, and find
examples of, the following features in the
text: fairly formal, impersonal style of
writing; the presentation and sequencing of
facts; the use of persuasive language and
opinions; the use of statistics, the use of the
present tense; the use of the third person; the
use of technical language and terms. *(There
are many possible examples.)*

### Sentence construction
### and punctuation

1 With the class, go through one of the sections
closely and identify the key points, writing
them down in note form on the board.
Without access to the text, ask the children
to write a summary of the section, using only
the brief notes on the board. Ask them to
then undertake this exercise on their own
with another of the sections. *(Answers will
depend on the section chosen.)*

## WORD Level
### Spelling

1 Select a range of words from the text which
have been suffixed, such as 'killed', 'bicycling'
and 'punishments'. *(There are many possible
examples.)* Ask the children to identify the root
word, explain how the suffix has changed its
meaning, and to comment on whether the
addition of the suffix has changed the spelling
of the root word in any way.

### Vocabulary extension

1 Provide the children with a starter list of
useful 'argument' words and phrases, such as
'although', 'reasons', 'point of view',
'furthermore', 'therefore', 'moreover', 'because',
'argument', 'support', 'evidence', 'statistic',
'persuade', 'advantages', 'disadvantages',
'conclusion', 'whereas', 'on the other hand',
'similarly', 'opinion', 'beliefs', etc. Encourage
the children to learn to spell these and
encourage them to incorporate them in their
own writing. Ask for further suggestions and
extend the list.

### Related texts:

'We're Talking about Alcohol' by Jenny Bryan

Books on safety/keeping safe:
'At Home' by Elizabeth Clark
'On My Own' by Anne Smith
'Take Care at Home' by Carole Wale

Personal safety:
'Feeling Happy, Feeling Safe' by Michele Elliott
'Look Out for Strangers' by Paul Humphrey
Road safety:
'Look Out on the Road' by Paul Humphrey
'Take Care on the Road' by Carole Wale

# Moonfleet

## *About the text*

*John Trenchard is trapped in the vaults of a church, hiding from smugglers amongst the coffins. When they finally leave, he drops his candle and, in the ensuing dark, is beset with panicky thoughts and feelings...*

## Teaching opportunities at:

### TEXT Level
### *Reading comprehension*

**1** Read the introduction and briefly flesh it out to set the passage in an appropriate context for the children.

**2** Explain that the children might not understand every word, and that some of the expressions and ways they are spoken are rather unusual because of when they were written. Read the passage through once as a whole to give children the gist of the extract. Ask them to recount the bones of the passage.

**3** Ask the children their opinion of it and to describe what sort of text it is – whether ghost, animal, adventure, etc.

**4** Discuss the setting. What sort of things might you expect in a setting like this? What features of the vaults might you expect to see? Encourage the children to read between the lines and use their imagination. What sort of picture do the children think the author conjures up? How? *(Focus on the dramatic use of adjectives.)*

**5** How does the author succeed in building up the tension of the story? *(He places it in the dark, and plays on the idea of touching without seeing, then of suddenly seeing something horrible. The language is very dramatic and suggestive.)* Ask the children to identify the

**Key Stage 2**
**Literacy Poster Pack 6**
**Letts EDUCATIONAL**

**Moonfleet**
*It is the 1700s. John Trenchard is trapped in the vaults of the church, hiding from smugglers. When they leave, he tries to make his escape.*

Thus, sitting where I was, I lit my candle once more, and then clambered across that great coffin which, for two hours or more, had been a mid-wall of partition between me and danger. But to get out of the niche was harder than to get in; for now that I had a candle to light me, I saw that the coffin, though sound enough to outer view, was wormed through and through, and little better than a rotten shell. So it was that I had some ado to get over it, not daring either to kneel upon it or to bring much weight to bear with my hand, lest it should go through. And now having got safely across, I sat for an instant on that narrow ledge of the stone shelf which projected beyond the coffin on the vault side, and made ready to jump forward onto the floor below. And how it happened I know not, but there I lost my balance, and as I slipped the candle flew out of my grasp. Then I clutched at the coffin to save myself, but my hand went clean through it, and so I came to the ground in a cloud of dust and splinters; having only got hold of a wisp of seaweed, or a handful of those draggled funeral trappings which were strewn about this place. The floor of the vault was sandy; and so, though I fell crookedly, I took but little harm beyond the shaking; and soon,

pulling myself together, set to strike my flint and blow the match into a flame to search for the fallen candle. Yet all the time I kept in my fingers this handful of light stuff; and when the flame burnt up again I held the thing against the light, and saw that it was no wisp of seaweed, but something black and wiry. For a moment, I could not gather what I had hold of, but then gave a start that nearly sent the candle out, and perhaps a cry, and let it drop as if it were red-hot iron, for I knew that it was a man's beard.

Now when I saw that, I felt a sort of throttling fright, as though one had caught hold of my heartstrings; and so many and such strange thoughts rose in me, that the blood went pounding round and round in my head, as it did once afterwards when I was fighting with the sea and near drowned. Surely to have in hand the beard of any dead man in any place was bad enough, but worse a thousand times in such a place as this, and to know on whose face it had grown. For, almost before I fully saw what it was, I knew it was that black beard which had given Colonel John Mohune his nickname, and that was his coffin I had hid behind.

J. Meade Faulkner

© Letts Educational 1998          **See *Letts Literacy Activity Book 6*  page 42**

sequence of main events in the passage. *(He has to get out of the vault – he lights a candle – he reaches a ledge – he drops the candle – he puts his hand through a rotten coffin – he falls to the ground clutching something – he relights the candle – he nearly faints when he realises he is holding human beard hair.)*

**6** How does the author describe John's feelings when he discovers what he had hold of? *(Absolute horror as the blood pounds round his head.)* How did this make the children feel? Why?

**7** Note that the story is written in the first-person. How does this manage to make it even more spooky? *(It makes it easier to experience the same feelings as the author and to empathise more fully.)*

## Writing composition

**1** Use this episode as a basis for stimulating some similar writing in the same genre. Ask the children to imagine they have been exploring a cave with a torch when drug smugglers come in to stash away their cargo. As they lie there in the dark and damp, they should be aware of strange movements and sounds all around, yet unable to do anything until the smugglers leave. Their imagination runs riot and as soon as the drug smugglers leave, they grab a torch and…

## SENTENCE Level
### Grammatical awareness

**1** Go through the text, pausing and discussing the use of language and any unusual ways of expressing things. Ask the children to write them in the sort of language we would use today. *(For example, 'So it was that I had some ado to get over it' could be written as 'Because of this, I had some difficulty getting over it'. There are many possible examples.)*

### Sentence construction and punctuation

**1** Some of the sentences are very long and complicated, such as the first sentence. Discuss how these could be broken down into shorter, simpler sentences. Select some more for the children to practise on and compare different versions. Does this have an effect on the drama of the text?

## WORD Level
### Spelling

**1** Identify and list some polysyllabic words from the text containing double consonants. Say them and work out how many syllables each consists of. Remind the children that where there is a double consonant, the syllable boundary falls between the consonants. Ask them to practise syllabifying the words in the list. *('Sit/ting', 'cof/fin', 'lit/tle', 'bet/ter', 'rot/ten', 'nar/row', 'hap/pened', 'slip/ped', 'drag/gled', 'trap/pings', 'pul/ling', 'fal/len', 'throt/tling' and 'ful/ly'.)* Look for other polysyllabic words of this kind in other reading books, too.

### Vocabulary extension

**1** Go through the text, discussing the use of language and any unusual words or expressions, encouraging the children to suggest what they might mean by using context and grammatical clues. Are there any words used that we rarely use today or use in a different way? *(For example 'ado', 'gave a start', 'trappings', etc.)* Suggest they check the meanings by using a dictionary.

---

### Related texts:

Suggested titles for smuggler-based stories:

'Spike and the Smugglers' by Deborah van der Beek

'Smugglers Bay' by Fiona Kelly

'The Great Elephant Chase' by Gillian Cross (a story about two children smuggling an elephant across America

# The War of the Worlds

## *About the text*

*This is an extract from an early sci-fi classic by H. G. Wells, which foretold of aliens landing on Earth long before the advent of space travel.*

## Teaching opportunities at:

### TEXT Level
### *Reading comprehension*

**1** Look at the title, introduction and illustration. What sort of story is it likely to be? *(It is a sci-fi story.)* Ask the children what sorts of things they expect to happen in these types of stories and what sorts of characters they are likely to come across.

**2** Read the text to and with the class. How does it fulfil the children's predictions in terms of plot and characters?

**3** What response does the story evoke in the reader? Ask the children to try to articulate and describe their feelings after reading it. Did they empathise with the main character?

**4** Reread the passage, pausing at appropriate places to discuss the unfolding of the story and the effect the events increasingly have on the main character as the alien emerges, forcing the writer radically to change his view of what he expected the being to be like.

**5** Discuss the way the author builds up the suspense as the alien emerges by slowly revealing the appearance of the being and by the drama of everybody's response to it.

**6** Draw attention to the powerful adjectives used to describe the alien and the feelings of the man. Does the fact that it is written in the first-person make the episode any more horrific? *(Discuss how this enables the writer to follow the shifting thoughts and observations of the character in graphic detail.)*

**Key Stage 2**
**Literacy Poster Pack 6**

*Letts*
EDUCATIONAL

### The War of the Worlds
*The writer is watching as an alien, which has just landed on Earth, comes out of its spacecraft.*

The end of the cylinder was being screwed out from within. Nearly two feet of shining screw projected. Somebody blundered against me, and I narrowly missed being pitched onto the top of the screw. I turned, and as I did so the screw must have come out, and the lid of the cylinder fell upon the gravel with a ringing concussion. I stuck my elbow into the person behind me and turned my head towards the Thing again. For a moment that circular cavity seemed perfectly black. I had the sunset in my eyes.

I think everyone expected to see a man emerge – possibly something a little unlike us terrestrial men, but in all essentials a man. I know I did. But, looking, I presently saw something stirring within the shadow – greyish billowy movements, one above another, and then two luminous discs like eyes. Then something resembling a little grey snake, about the thickness of a walking-stick, coiled up out of the writhing middle, and wriggled in the air towards me – and then another.

A sudden chill came over me. There was a loud shriek from a woman behind.

I half turned, keeping my eyes fixed upon the cylinder still, from which other tentacles were now projecting, and began pushing my way back from the edge of the pit. I found myself alone, and saw the people on the other side of the pit running off ... I looked again at the cylinder, and ungovernable terror gripped me. I stood petrified and staring.

A big, greyish, rounded bulk, the size perhaps of a bear, was rising slowly and painfully out of the cylinder. As it bulged up and caught the light, it glistened like wet leather. Two large dark-coloured eyes were regarding me steadfastly. It was rounded, and had, one might say, a face. There was a mouth under the eyes, the lipless rim of which quivered and panted, and dropped saliva. The body heaved and pulsated convulsively. A lank tentacular appendage gripped the edge of the cylinder, another swayed in the air.

H. G. Wells

© Letts Educational 1998    See *Letts Literacy Activity Book 6*  page 48

**7** Ask the children to read each paragraph separately and to write just one sentence saying what is happening in each. *(For example, the mysterious cylinder opens – something with tentacles emerges – more appears – finally, the whole, hideous thing appears.)*

### *Writing composition*

**1** Encourage the children to produce an extended piece of sci-fi writing along similar lines, perhaps an invasion by aliens, as part of a class anthology of such stories. Encourage them to plan, redraft and bring their stories to a presentational standard, considering aspects of layout, paragraphing, accuracy of punctuation and spelling, handwriting or printing.

## SENTENCE Level
### Grammatical awareness

**1** Use the passage as a basis for reviewing work on word classes. Select one particular class of word at a time, e.g. nouns. Read through the passage and identify all the nouns. *(There are many possible examples.)* Ask the children to say whether they are singular or plural, common, proper, abstract or collective, etc. Apply the same sort of approach to other classes of words, such as verbs, adjectives, adverbs, pronouns, prepositions, etc. Whilst undertaking this, discuss the author's selection of words and how effective the children think they are.

### Sentence construction and punctuation

**1** The theme of the passage is a good vehicle for introducing work on conditional words and phrases like 'if… then', 'might', 'could' and 'would', in speculation and supposition. *(These are clauses or sentences which express the idea that the occurrence of one thing depends on another.)* Encourage the children to make up conditional sentences based on the alien theme perhaps 'If the creature came any nearer, it might grab me', 'The cylinder could contain an alien' or 'What would the strange being do next?', etc.

## WORD Level
### Spelling

**1** Find the words in the text with the following common word endings: '-ous', '-ssion', '-ial', '-ment', '-able', '-dge', '-ar', '-age'. *('-ous': 'luminous', 'tumultuous', 'tedious'; '-ssion': 'concussion'; '-ial': 'terrestrial', 'essential'; '-ment': 'moment', 'movement'; '-able': 'ungovernable'; '-dge': 'edge', 'ridge', 'wedge'; '-ar': 'war', 'circular', 'bear', 'tentacular', 'peculiar'; '-age': 'appendage'.)* Ask the children to suggest some other words containing the same letter patterns. List them and use them for spelling practice.

**2** Find some words containing silent letters. *(For example 'writhing' and 'glistened'.)* Ask the children to suggest some other words containing silent letters (not just 'w' and 't'). They might look in books for other ideas.

**3** 'Saliva' is an interesting word to discuss because it ends in 'a'. Brainstorm a list of other words that end in a consonant plus a vowel (other than 'e').

### Vocabulary extension

**1** There are many unusual words in the text. Select some and ask the children to suggest their meanings by reference to the passage and by using dictionaries. *(You might start with 'appendages' and 'cavity'.)*

**2** Notice the use of the word 'presently', the meaning of which has changed over time. Discuss what it means in the context of the passage. *(In this context it means 'immediately', though the modern meaning is 'soon' or 'at the moment'.)* Consider other words like 'nice' and 'without' and ask the children to discover and list how their meanings have changed, too.

> ### Related texts:
> Other 'alien' books:
> 'Alien Attack' by Michael Johnstone
> 'Alien Dawn' by M. Pearson
> 'Alien Invasion' by Christopher Pyke
> 'Grinny' by Nicholas Fisk

# The Eagle of the Ninth

## About the text

*This extract is set in Ancient Britain during the Roman occupation and is written by Rosemary Sutcliff.*

## Teaching opportunities at:

### TEXT Level
### Reading comprehension

1 Before reading the text, read the introduction. Ask the class to share any knowledge they have of the Romans. To set the passage in context, explain the role slave labour had in sustaining the Roman Empire by providing the raw labour for building projects, as household servants, and as gladiators for the Romans' entertainment in the arena. Slaves were generally held in fairly low esteem – their lives were virtually worthless. Slaves were often 'barbarians' captured in Roman conquests.

2 Read the passage all the way through to the children to give them the gist of the passage, irrespective of whether some of the 'Roman' words are understood or not.

3 Read it through a second time, pausing to discuss any unfamiliar or unknown words, to ask the children to guess their meaning or to refer to dictionaries for clarification.

4 Ask the children to consider how the author creates a sense of curiosity and expectation in the first paragraph. Do the children want to read on? *(It is a thoughtful passage, with the character introducing some unanswered questions.)*

5 How can you tell it was quiet in the atrium where Marcus was sitting? How can you tell that he was waiting expectantly for the slave to come? *(We can infer it is quiet because*

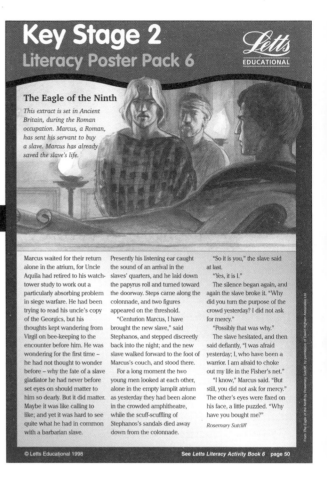

## Key Stage 2
### Literacy Poster Pack 6

Letts EDUCATIONAL

**The Eagle of the Ninth**

*This extract is set in Ancient Britain, during the Roman occupation. Marcus, a Roman, has sent his servant to buy a slave. Marcus has already saved the slave's life.*

Marcus waited for their return alone in the atrium, for Uncle Aquila had retired to his watch-tower study to work out a particularly absorbing problem in siege warfare. He had been trying to read his uncle's copy of the Georgics, but his thoughts kept wandering from Virgil on bee-keeping to the encounter before him. He was wondering for the first time – he had not thought to wonder before – why the fate of a slave gladiator he had never before set eyes on should matter to him so dearly. But it did matter. Maybe it was like calling to like; and yet it was hard to see quite what he had in common with a barbarian slave.

Presently his listening ear caught the sound of an arrival in the slaves' quarters, and he laid down the papyrus roll and turned toward the doorway. Steps came along the colonnade, and two figures appeared on the threshold.

"Centurion Marcus, I have brought the new slave," said Stephanos, and stepped discreetly back into the night; and the new slave walked forward to the foot of Marcus's couch, and stood there.

For a long moment the two young men looked at each other, alone in the empty lamplit atrium as yesterday they had been alone in the crowded amphitheatre, while the scuff-scuffling of Stephanos's sandals died away down from the colonnade.

"So it is you," the slave said at last.

"Yes, it is I."

The silence began again, and again the slave broke it. "Why did you turn the purpose of the crowd yesterday? I did not ask for mercy."

"Possibly that was why."

The slave hesitated, and then said defiantly, "I was afraid yesterday; I, who have been a warrior. I am afraid to choke out my life in the Fisher's net."

"I know," Marcus said. "But still, you did not ask for mercy." The other's eyes were fixed on his face, a little puzzled. "Why have you bought me?"

*Rosemary Sutcliff*

© Letts Educational 1998      **See *Letts Literacy Activity Book 6*  page 50**

*Marcus waits alone and he catches the sound of the slave's arrival in the distance. It is the sound he is waiting for expectantly.)*

6 What does the way Stephanos addresses Marcus tell us about him (Marcus)? *(He is a centurion, and treated respectfully by Stephanos.)*

7 Ask the children to suggest how Marcus had saved the slave's life in the amphitheatre the day before. How could Marcus and the slave have 'been alone in the busy amphitheatre'? Why is the slave puzzled by Marcus' behaviour? *(He treated him leniently and is not behaving as a slave master might.)*

8 What clues are there in the text that this is a historical novel, set in Roman times? *(Look at the introduction, the illustration, the references to 'atrium', 'Georgics', 'Virgil', 'barbarian slave', 'centurions', the characters' names, 'amphitheatre', etc.)*

## Writing composition

1 Marcus saved his slave's life. Write a sequel to this story in which the slave saves Marcus' life and is given his freedom. Discuss appropriate names for the slave. Discuss possible scenarios: perhaps when sailing back to Rome, there is a shipwreck; whilst out hunting, Marcus is cornered by a wild boar, etc. If appropriate, encourage the children to do some research on the Roman period, especially on master/slave relationships, before attempting any writing.

## SENTENCE Level
### Grammatical awareness

1 The text is full of complex sentences. Ask the children to rewrite some of them in simpler, shorter sentences, without losing the meaning. Suggest that the first part might be written along the lines of 'Marcus was alone in the atrium. He was waiting for Stephanos and the slave to return', etc.

### Sentence construction and punctuation

1 Ask the children to write and explain the function of the following, by reference to examples in the text: dashes; semi-colons; apostrophes. *(They are used for pauses, for lists, for contractions and to indicate possession, respectively.)*

## WORD Level
### Spelling

1 Find the examples of words with a soft 'g' ('Virgil') and soft 'c' ('centurion') in the text. After a class discussion, list other such words to learn by looking in other reading books.

2 Find some words in the text that begin with 'wa-' or 'wo-'. *('Wa-': 'wanted', 'watch', 'warfare', 'wandering', 'was', 'walked', 'warrior', 'war'; 'wo-': 'work', 'wonder[ing]', 'wonder'.)* By reference to dictionaries, list some other words. Ask the children to categorise the words according to the way the 'a' or 'o' is pronounced in each.

### Vocabulary extension

1 List all the words in the text that have Roman connections. *('Atrium', 'Georgics', 'Virgil', 'gladiator', 'slave', 'papyrus', 'colonnade', 'centurion', 'couch', 'amphitheatre', 'sandals' and 'Fisher's net'.)* Ask the children to write the meaning of each by reference to a dictionary or encylopedia.

### Related texts:

Other titles by Rosemary Sutcliff:

'The Light Beyond the Forest'

'The Armourer's House'

'Shining Company'

'Knight's Fee'

'The Witch's Brat'

'Beowulf: Dragon Slayer'

Information books on Roman Britain:

'Roman Britain' by Jenny Hall

'The Romans in Britain' by Dorothy Metcalf

# Water Supplies

## About the text

*This information text details the essential nature of water, together with the provision of statistics about water safety throughout the world.*

## Teaching opportunities at:

### TEXT Level
### Reading comprehension

**1** Read the article through completely once, to give the children the gist. What is the main message of the article? *(The importance of the availability of clean, fresh water.)* Ask the children to try and explain what 'adequate safe water supplies and sanitation' means. (Use a dictionary, if necessary.) Discuss the fact that while we take the provision of these things for granted, many people in the world cannot.

**2** Now read the article again, pausing after each section for discussion about the following points:

• After reading the first section, ask the children to identify the key ideas. In note form, record these on the board. *(For example, each year 5 million people die from poor water supplies – water covers 70% of the earth's surface – most is salty – fresh water is spread unevenly across the Earth.)* What inference do children draw from the statistics on average water?

• After reading 'Using water', ask what the most important use of water is. *(It sustains animal and human life.)* Ask the children to discuss their reactions to the statistics about the water content of bodies. Encourage the children to elaborate the bullet-pointed list by suggesting examples of the way water is used for each.

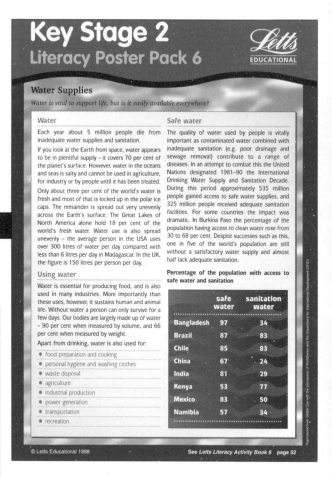

• Read the 'Safe water' section. Study carefully the construction of this paragraph with the children. *(It begins with establishing the main point. It sets out an example of what is being done and its results. Finally it sets the situation in a realistic context.)*

**3** Study and discuss the statistical chart. Ask some guided questions to help focus, such as 'Which country listed has most/least access to safe water and sanitation?', 'Which country is best/worst overall?', etc.

**4** Finally, review and reflect on how well this article presents some of the following features of a balanced argument: the clear expression, sequencing and linkage of points; the provision of persuasive examples, and evidence, e.g. statistics; and appealing to the assumed views and feelings of the reader.

## Writing composition

1 Ask the children to write a summary or commentary on the article, stating just the main points, and crediting the views expressed by using expressions such as 'The writer says that…'

2 Ask the children to write a balanced report on a controversial issue, such as homework, summarising fairly the competing views and analysing the strengths and weaknesses of different positions. Before doing this, ask the children to make rough notes on the arguments for and against to marshal their thoughts. It might be helpful to suggest a framework structure to work within, like 'Some people think that… because… they argue that… However, on the other hand… disagree with the idea that… They argue that… They also say… My view is that… because…'

## SENTENCE Level
### Grammatical awareness

1 Identify examples of active and passive verbs in the text. Practise changing them from one form to another, noting changes in word order and meaning. (So 'The average person in the USA uses over 300 litres of water per day' [active] becomes 'Over 300 litres of water per day are used by the average person in the USA' [passive]. There are many examples to choose from.)

## Sentence construction and punctuation

1 Link this with the work on composition on note-taking and writing summaries, showing how sentences may be contracted.

## WORD Level
### Spelling

1 Ask the children to find a given number of words in the text, say ten, that have been prefixed or suffixed. (There are many possible examples.) Identify the root word in each case, noting how its spelling and meaning has been affected, if at all. Also ask the children to identify what class of word each root word is, whether it is a noun, adjective, verb, pronoun, etc.

## Vocabulary extension

1 Provide the children with a number of relevant proverbs. (For example, 'Waste not, want not', 'We never miss the water till the well runs dry', 'Still waters run deep', etc.) Ask them to explain what they think they mean.

2 Extend this by giving them beginnings and endings of other well-known proverbs to match up. If possible, refer to dictionaries of proverbs and other reference sources to try to discover their origins.

### Related texts:

'Keeping Water Clean' by Ewan McLeigh

'Water and Life' by Barbara Taylor

'Water at Work' by Barbara Taylor

'Troubled Waters' by Dennis Leggett

'What We Can Do About Wasting Water' by Donna Bailey

Safety near water title:

'Near Water' by Anne Smith

# The Phantom Tollbooth

## About the text

*Milo and his dog find themselves in the Kingdom of Dictionopolis, from where all the words in the world come.*

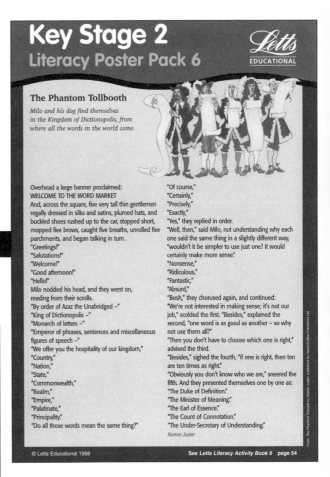

## Teaching opportunities at:

### TEXT Level
#### Reading comprehension

1 Read the passage to the class. Ask the children to volunteer their immediate opinions and responses to it in general. Did they like it? Find it amusing? Silly? Strange?

2 What do children understand a 'word market' to be? Remind them of the introduction for a clue.

3 Who greets Milo and his dog? *(Five thin gentlemen.)* How are they dressed? *(In fine silks, satins, plumes and buckles.)* What might the way they are dressed indicate? *(That they are educated and wealthy.)* What is strange about the way they greet Milo? *(They take it in turns to speak, each offering a different word with the same meaning.)*

4 Ask the children if they think Milo was expected or not. Is there any evidence to support their views? *(The evidence that they expected him lies in the five men having prepared sheets from which to read.)*

5 In what way are the men like parrots? In what way are they different? *(Although they repeat each other, they do so using different words.)*

6 Ask the children to explain what a synonym is and what relevance that has to the extract. *(It is a word with a similar meaning.)*

7 Ask the children if they would find it frustrating or amusing to be in the Kingdom for long. Why?

8 Is it true to say that Milo argues for conciseness and brevity? *(Yes, by suggesting it would be simpler to use one word rather than five.)* What is the argument the five men use against this? *(They are not interested in making sense and it would be a waste of good words not to use them all.)*

### Writing composition

1 This story could be rewritten as a play, and continued. Perhaps Milo is taken to see the King – what conversation might he have with him? Remind the children of how a playscript is set out by looking again at Unit 1.6, 'The Wind in the Willows'.

**2** Ask the children to write a story in the same vein in which Milo visits the Land of Antonyms (opposites). What adventures could he have? Who would he meet? How would he cope?

**3** How would poetry be written in Dictionopolis or the Land of Antonyms? Pick a theme and brainstorm ideas. Why not try the exercise as a class first and then individually?

# SENTENCE Level
## Grammatical awareness

**1** The King is very interested in words. Apply this interest to a study of the passage, reviewing work on word classes. Select one particular class of word at a time, e.g. nouns. Read through the passage and identify all the nouns. *(There are many possible examples.)* Ask the children to say whether they are singular or plural, common, proper, abstract or collective, and what their gender is. Apply the same sort of approach to verbs. What tense are they? Are they active or passive? Look for examples of other classes of words, e.g. adjectives, adverbs, pronouns, prepositions and discuss their functions.

## Sentence construction and punctuation

**1** Record sections of the passage in indirect speech, taking the opportunity to contract and summarise at the same time, along the lines of 'The five men greeted Milo and welcomed him in various ways'.

**2** Try writing some personal responses to the passage using conditionals. *(For example, 'If I visited the Kingdom I would find it rather frustrating. I might get rather annoyed. I would tell the king that… ', etc.)*

# WORD Level
## Spelling

**1** The passage is full of words with common word endings. Find examples of the following: '-ment', '-tion', '-or', '-ous', '-ure', '-ealth', '-ate', '-ity', '-ly', '-nce' and '-ary'. *('-ment': 'parchment(s)'; '-tion': 'connotation', 'salutation(s)', 'nation', 'definition'; '-or': 'emperor'; '-ous': 'miscellaneous', 'ridiculous'; '-ure': 'figure(s)'; '-ealth': 'commonwealth'; '-ate': 'state', 'palatinate'; '-ity': 'hospitality', 'principality'; 'ly': 'regally', 'certainly', 'precisely', 'exactly', 'slightly', 'obviously'; '-nce': 'sentence(s)', 'essence'; '-ary': 'secretary'.)* Ask the children to supply at least three other words for each of these common word endings.

**2** Ask the children to volunteer some words they find tricky from the extract, such as 'miscellaneous'. Ask them for suggestions on how they could remember them. *(Underline difficult parts; say the words as they are written; make up silly sentences or mnemonics; look for smaller, known words inside each; use the 'Look, say, cover, write, check' method.)*

## Vocabulary extension

**1** The King of Dictionopolis would be very interested in all aspects of words and sayings. Collect some proverbs for a class collection. Ask the children to explain their meanings and suggest how they might have originated.

**2** Ask the children to suggest common expressions or idioms, such as 'to be a wet blanket'. What do they mean? How are they used? How might they have come about?

> ### Related texts:
> 'Word Origins' by George Beal
> 'Chambers Thesaurus – A Comprehensive Word-finding Dictionary' edited by Anne Seaton, George Davidson, Catherine Schwarz, Johns Simpson

## Children at Work

### *About the text*

*This is taken from a leaflet issued by the Child Accident Prevention Trust embodying advice and guidance couched in fairly formal language.*

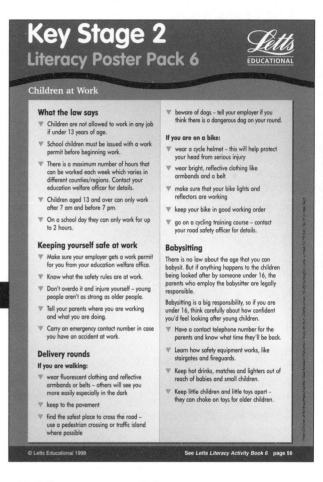

## Teaching opportunities at:

### TEXT Level
#### *Reading comprehension*

**1** Read the leaflet through once to and with the class. Discuss who the intended reader is – is it adults or young people? What evidence is there to support this view? *(It is aimed at children as it is written to 'you'.)*

**2** Discuss the 'What the law says' section. Ask the children if there is anything that surprises them? Is the law being obeyed? Is it fair? Why are there such laws?

**3** Ask the children to rank the points in the 'Keeping yourself safe at work' in order of importance and to justify their views.

**4** Look at the 'Delivery rounds' section. Ask the children to suggest what sort of delivery rounds it might be referring to. How is the section divided up? What do the children think of the advice offered? Is there any other advice that could have been included?

**5** Ask the children if, after reading the 'Babysitting' section, they feel there should be a minimum age for undertaking it. Encourage them to justify their views.

**6** Ask the children how helpful they think the leaflet is and why.

### *Writing composition*

**1** Suggest some scenarios that might happen whilst babysitting and ask the children to write what their sequence of responses would be in each case and why.

**2** Encourage the children to formulate a questionnaire, perhaps on a subject related to school life. Discuss the need for conciseness, specificity and directness in the language of the questions. Allow them to carry it out in the school and to assess the success and effectiveness of it.

## SENTENCE Level
### Grammatical awareness

1 Discuss the following features of some 'official' documents: subheadings; use of bold print; use of bullet-points; 'official', fairly formal, language which often contains technical terms and can be hard to understand; complicated sentences; imperative form of verbs; asterisks or footnotes; and few pictures. Which does this leaflet contain?

2 Collect some examples of other official documents and compare their features. Discuss why official forms tend to use a standard form of English, rather than a chatty, informal style.

### Sentence construction and punctuation

1 Study the sentences in the text. Identify which are one-clause sentences and which contain more than one clause. *(There are many possible examples.)* In the latter, decide which clause is the main clause, and which offer support or elaboration (subordinate clauses) – or are all clauses of equal importance? How could sentences with more than one clause be rewritten as two or more simple sentences?

## WORD Level
### Spelling

1 Identify and list some of the polysyllabic words from the text. *(There are many possible examples.)* Say them and work out how many syllables each consists of. Remind the children that where there is a double consonant, the syllable boundary falls between the consonants. *(For example, 'lit/tle'.)* Practise syllabifying the polysyllabic words and marking in syllable boundaries. Refer to dictionaries such as 'The Concise Oxford Dictionary' that show the syllabification of words and explain the marking conventions they use. Consider which of the syllables are stressed and unstressed in the words.

### Vocabulary extension

1 Ask the children to think of words, common expressions or proverbs containing the reference to people or animals. *(For example, 'babysitting', 'horseplay', 'throwing the baby out with the bath water', 'counting chickens before they are hatched', etc.)* Discuss what they mean and how they are used.

### Related texts:

Titles which look at other aspects of safety in everyday life:

'Take Care at Home' by Carole Wale
'Look Out on the Road' by Paul Humphrey
'Take Care on the Road' by Carole Wale
'Look Out for Strangers' by Paul Humphrey

See also – for care of children in Victorian times:

'A child in Victorian London' by Edwina Conner
'Growing Up in Victorian Days' by Molly Harrison

An excellent book to introduce here is the story of Jim Jarvis (the first Doctor Barnardo boy). The story illustrates a child's lot in the workhouses of Victorian England.
'Street Child' by Berlie Doherty

# Cinderilla

## *About the text*

*The story of Cinderella (as we now call her) has been around for a long time. This version of the story was first published in 1729.*

# Teaching opportunities at:

## TEXT Level

### *Reading comprehension*

1 Look at the title, introduction and illustration. Note, too, the spelling of 'Cinderilla'. Did the children realise the story was such an old one? Ask the children to recount the details of the story as they remember it. Will this story contain the same elements?

2 Read the extract. Ask the children to compare and contrast the characters of Cinderilla and her two stepsisters – in appearance, behaviour and the opportunities they each have.

3 Ask the children to discuss in what way the stepdaughters are like their mother. (*In brief, they are proud and vain.*)

4 Ask the children to explain what it means when it says 'As soon as the wedding was over, the new wife began to show her real character'? What is her real character? (*Answers will depend on the children's interpretation.*) How does she treat Cinderilla? (*Cruelly.*) Why? (*She is jealous and because she can.*)

5 The father is a fairly low-key figure in the story. Ask the children what can be inferred about him. What is his relationship like with his wife? Is there anything surprising about the way he allows Cinderilla to be treated?

6 Is Cinderilla her real name? (*No.*) How did she get it? (*Her step-sisters named her 'Cinderbreech' then 'Cinderilla' after her habit of quietly sitting by the chimney corner, among the cinders.*)

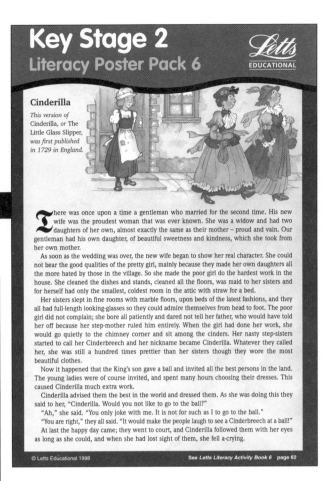

**Key Stage 2**
**Literacy Poster Pack 6**

*Letts*
EDUCATIONAL

### Cinderilla

*This version of Cinderilla, or The Little Glass Slipper, was first published in 1729 in England.*

There was once upon a time a gentleman who married for the second time. His new wife was the proudest woman that was ever known. She was a widow and had two daughters of her own, almost exactly the same as their mother – proud and vain. Our gentleman had his own daughter, of beautiful sweetness and kindness, which she took from her own mother.

As soon as the wedding was over, the new wife began to show her real character. She could not bear the good qualities of the pretty girl, mainly because they made her own daughters all the more hated by those in the village. So she made the poor girl do the hardest work in the house. She cleaned the dishes and stands, cleaned all the floors, was maid to her sisters and for herself had only the smallest, coldest room in the attic with straw for a bed.

Her sisters slept in fine rooms with marble floors, upon beds of the latest fashions, and they all had full-length looking-glasses so they could admire themselves from head to foot. The poor girl did not complain; she bore all patiently and dared not tell her father, who would have told her off because her step-mother ruled him entirely. When the girl had done her work, she would go quietly to the chimney corner and sit among the cinders. Her nasty step-sisters started to call her Cinderbreech and her nickname became Cinderilla. Whatever they called her, she was still a hundred times prettier than her sisters though they wore the most beautiful clothes.

Now it happened that the King's son gave a ball and invited all the best persons in the land. The young ladies were of course invited, and spent many hours choosing their dresses. This caused Cinderilla much extra work.

Cinderilla advised them the best in the world and dressed them. As she was doing this they said to her, "Cinderilla. Would you not like to go to the ball?"

"Ah," she said. "You only joke with me. It is not for such as I to go to the ball."

"You are right," they all said. "It would make the people laugh to see a Cinderbreech at a ball!"

At last the happy day came; they went to court, and Cinderilla followed them with her eyes as long as she could, and when she had lost sight of them, she fell a-crying.

© Letts Educational 1998
**See Letts Literacy Activity Book 6   page 62**

7 Don't the children think it extraordinary that Cinderilla does not hate her step-sisters? Why does she fall 'a-crying' at the end?

8 How did the story match up to the children's expectations? (*Explain that there are two more poster versions of the story to compare this with later.*)

### *Writing composition*

1 Ask the children to rewrite the extract from the point of view of one of the other characters, perhaps the step-mother, one of the step-sisters or the father, keeping to the style of the original as closely as possible.

2 The extract could be turned into a playscript, and set out accordingly with a part for a narrator, stage directions, etc. When it has been drafted, perform it in class and see if it can be improved in any way.

# SENTENCE Level
## Grammatical awareness

**1** Study the narrative text and draw out some of its language conventions and grammatical features. Ask the children to find examples of the following in the text: predictable expressions and connectives used to structure and sequence the story: 'Once upon a time', 'As soon as', 'Now it happened', 'At last', etc.; use of paragraphs each with separate idea, moving the story on; fairly long and complex sentences; written in the third-person; past tense verbs; and use of dialogue.

## Sentence construction and punctuation

**1** Provide the children with some simple one-clause sentences based on the text. Ask them to make the sentences into complex sentences by adding additional clauses. *('Cinderilla was the only daughter of the old man' could become 'Cinderilla, who was a kind and sweet girl, was the only daughter of the old man' or 'The old man had one daughter called Cinderilla, who was kind and sweet'.)*

# WORD Level
## Spelling

**1** Use the following nouns from the text: 'dish', 'daughter', 'wife' and 'lady'. Ask the children to write them in the plural. *('Dishes', 'daughters', 'wives' and 'ladies'.)* Ask the children to note what happens. Provide them with a variety of other words to pluralise: regular words that just take 's'; words ending in 'sh' (dish), 'ch' (stitch), 'x' (fox) that take 'es'; words ending in consonant plus 'y' (lady, fairy) in which the 'y' is changed to 'i' and 'es' is added; words that end in 'f' or 'fe' (shelf, wife) in which the 'f' changes to 'v' and 'es' is added.

**2** Ask the children to sort the words into groups according to how they are pluralised and to make up rules to cover each type.

## Vocabulary extension

**1** Use the nouns 'sweetness and kindness' from the text to show how verbs can be made into nouns by the addition of a suffix. Provide children with a range of common noun endings, e.g. '-ness', '-tion', '-ment', '-ance', '-iour', '-ure', '-dom', etc. Provide them with a list of verbs (perhaps taken from the text) such as 'marry', 'hate', 'clean', etc. Ask them to have fun making up their own nouns by adding suffixes, e.g. 'marriment', 'hatedom', 'cleaniour', etc.

### Related texts:

'Children's Fairytale Theatre: Three Plays to Perform: Cinderella, Beauty and the Beast, Aladdin' by Terri Wiltshire

'Little Red Riding Hood' by Moira Butterfield

'Puss in Boots (Play Tales)' by Moira Butterfield

# Cinderella

## *About the text*

*This version of Cinderella by Roald Dahl is not the same gentle creature as in the traditional story!*

## Teaching opportunities at:

### TEXT Level
### *Reading comprehension*

**1** Read the poem to and with the class to encourage the children to give their immediate responses and impressions. What sort of a poem is it? Did they like it? Why or why not? What particularly struck them about it?

**2** Ask the children to describe how Cinderella is portrayed. What sort of a girl is she? How does she behave? What words could be used to describe her? Use evidence from the poem to justify their views. How does she compare with the previous version of Cinderilla in, Unit 3.1?

**3** How can you tell this is a modern version? Which words or phrases show this? *(There is a disco rather than a ball at the palace and she wants to wear nylon panty-hose.)*

**4** Is the Magic Fairy different from the usual stereotype? How? *(Although she uses her wand to work the spell, she speaks in modern language: 'Hang on a tick'.)*

**5** How did Cinderella's appearance affect the Ugly Sisters? *(It made them wince.)*

**6** How did the Prince respond to Cinderella's approach? *(He was turned to pulp and could not resist her firm advances!)*

**7** How is the structure of this text different from the previous one? *(This is a poem, in rhyming verse.)*

Key Stage 2
Literacy Poster Pack 6
Letts EDUCATIONAL

Cinderella
This modern Cinderella is not quite the same gentle creature as in the traditional story.

She bellowed "Help!" and "Let me out!"
The Magic Fairy heard her shout.
Appearing in a blaze of light,
She said, "My dear, are you all right?"
"All right?" cried Cindy. "Can't you see
I feel as rotten as can be!"
She beat her fist against the wall,
And shouted, "Get me to the Ball!
There is a Disco at the Palace!
The rest have gone and I am jealous!
I want a dress! I want a coach!
And earrings and a diamond brooch!
And silver slippers, two of those!
And lovely nylon panty-hose!
Done up like that I'll guarantee
The handsome Prince will fall for me!"
The Fairy said, "Hang on a tick,"
She gave her wand a mighty flick
And quickly, in no time at all,
Cindy was at the Palace Ball!
It made the Ugly Sisters wince
To see her dancing with the Prince.
She held him very tight and pressed
herself against his manly chest.
The Prince himself was turned to pulp,
All he could do was gasp and gulp.
*Roald Dahl*

© Letts Educational 1998    See *Letts Literacy Activity Book 6*  page 64

## *Writing composition*

**1** Ask the children to continue the story in the same vein as the poem. They should try to keep the rhyming working and to keep the same funny tone.

**2** Make a poster, or design a book blurb, about the poem, trying to persuade people to read it. Briefly highlight its good points, and tempt and tantalise people by offering snippets to whet their appetites and leave them wanting more. Use persuasive phrases or words like 'Miss it at your peril!' and so on.

## SENTENCE Level
### Grammatical awareness

1 The poem involves playing with words for effect. Use the poem as a basis for reviewing work on word classes. Select one particular class of word at a time, e.g. nouns. Read through the poem and identify all the nouns. *(There are many possible examples.)* Ask the children to say whether they are singular or plural, common, proper, abstract or collective, and what their gender is. Apply the same sort of approach to verbs. What tense are they? Are they active or passive? There are many powerful verbs in the poem. Consider their effectiveness. Look for examples of other classes of words, such as adjectives, adverbs, pronouns, prepositions and discuss their functions.

### Sentence construction and punctuation

1 Identify, name and explain the functions of each punctuation mark in the poem. *(Speech marks, exclamation marks, full stops, commas, capitals, question marks, apostrophes for contraction and hyphens.)* Ask the children to explain any special conventions associated with them, for instance, the conventions associated with the use of speech marks. How does each punctuation mark offer help to the reader?

## WORD Level
### Spelling

1 Find the example of a soft 'g' word *('gentle')* and soft 'c' words *('prince', 'Cindy', 'palace', 'wince' and 'dancing')* in the poem. Ask the children to suggest ten other examples in each category. Invent some rules for when to use a soft 'g' or 'c'.

2 Find the word 'guarantee' in the poem. Use a dictionary to find other words beginning with 'gu' and followed by another vowel. List ten and make up a rule explaining why the 'g' has to be followed by the 'u'. *(We use the 'u' as a 'wall' to stop the 'g' from making a soft sound.)*

### Vocabulary extension

1 Have fun with the poem, rewriting it and deliberately misspelling words for effect. *(For example, 'She belowed "Help!" and "Leave it out!" the Magick Furry herd her showt'.)*

### Related texts:

Stories by Roald Dahl in play form:
'Roald Dahl's Charlie and the Great Glass Elevator: A Play' by Roald Dahl
'Fantastic Mr Fox; A Play/Adapted by Sally Reid' by Roald Dahl

Other poems:
'Rhyme Stew' by Roald Dahl
'Roald Dahl's Revolting Rhymes'

## Computerella

Unfortunately, the publishers of 'Computerella' would not grant permission for the text to be reproduced in poster form. The accompanying poster, therefore, consists of the illustration from *Letts Literacy Book 6*. This may be used as a stimulus to discuss what form a modern version of Cinderella might take and, as a writing activity, to write a playscript or part of a playscript on this theme. However, the poster could also be used alongside the actual text in the Activity Book. In this way, the ideas below are equally relevant and may be used just as effectively.

### *About the text*

*This modern version of Cinderella, in the form of a play, takes a quirky look at how the fairy Godmother might behave today. It provides a further version of the story for comparing and contrasting.*

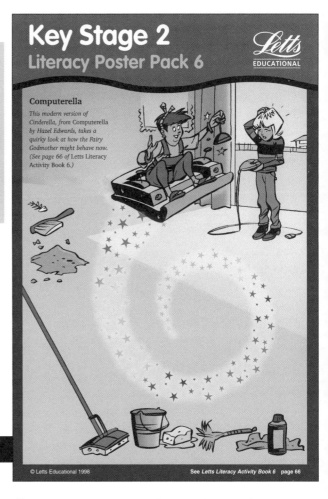

## Teaching opportunities at:

### TEXT Level
### *Reading comprehension*

**1** Look at the title, introduction and illustration as a class. Glance briefly at the layout of the text. Ask the children how they feel this text will differ from the previous two. *(It is a playscript rather than a story or poem, and is set in the computer age.)* How can they tell what type of text it is? *(The dialogue has no speech marks and is always preceded by the name of the character who is speaking. There is a narrator and there are stage directions.)* What sort of things might happen in it?

**2** Read the text to and with the class and ask the children for the gist of the text. *(Ella is too busy to fix the Prince's computer as she has to cook and clean for her sisters. Her fairy Godmother helps with a speed-clean so Ella can go to the Palace.)*

**3** In what sense are Ella's problems the same as in the traditional version? *(Her sisters make her work while they have all the fun.)*

**4** How is the Fairy Godmother different in this version? *(She is an 'Electronic Godmother'.)* How can you tell Ella has never seen her before? *(Ella says, 'Oh, I've heard about you.')* What is her magic 'wand'? *(It is a joystick.)* What sort of things does she do? *(She uses her joystick to fast-forward the work and then to produce computer disks and a mouse.)*

**5** What message has Ella received from the Palace? What is the problem there? *(The Prince's computer is broken and they ask Ella to fix it.)* By inference, work out what special skills Ella has. *(She is highly skilled working with electronics and computers.)* Why do you think Ella's Godmother provides her with some computer disks and a mouse and tells her she might need them? *(They are the attachments that will help to fix the Prince's computer.)*

**6** Do the children think the title is an apt one for the play? Why do they think that? *(Answers will depend on the children's interpretations.)*

**7** Ask the children to suggest what might happen next. Do they think Ella fixes the Prince's computer or not? What if she doesn't?

## Writing composition

**1** Ask the children to compare the three versions of Cinderella in writing. Encourage them to consider how the style of presentation of the three stories is different. Who wrote each version? *(The first is a traditional retelling, the second poem is by Roald Dahl and the third is by Hazel Edwards.)* In what way are the themes of each the same? *(For example, exploitation, magic intervention, good triumphing over bad, etc.)* How do the children think each writer portrays Cinderella. Consider how the setting for each is different. *(There is both the old-fashioned and the modern represented.)* What do they think were the strengths and weaknesses of each? How successful were they in what they set out to do? Which set out to be serious and which funny? What was the target audience for each? How did they aim to appeal to the reader? Which was most appealing? Why? *(All the answers will depend on the children's interpretation.)*

## SENTENCE Level
### Grammatical awareness

**1** Rewrite a section of the play, experimenting with changing the word order in sentences, changing verbs from active to passive, joining short sentences and making longer ones, etc., whilst still retaining the basic meaning. *(For example, 'Poor Ella. Her sisters made her work so hard' might become 'The floor is being swept by Ella, who is looking very sad'.)*

## Sentence construction and punctuation

**1** Explore the use of conditionals in the past and future, based on the story. Speculate on possible causes why Ella is in the situation she is in – perhaps Ella has been told off by her sisters; she might have been younger than them, etc. Review a range of possible future outcomes using conditionals, such as 'Ella might fix the prince's computer' and 'They might fall in love', etc.

## WORD Level
### Spelling

**1** Find some words in the text with the following endings: '-ic', '-en', '-age', '-ace', '-kin', '-ear', '-ern'. *('-ic': 'electronic'; '-en': 'olden'; '-age': 'message'; '-ace': 'Palace'; '-kin': 'pumpkin(s)'; '-ear': 'appear'; '-ern': 'modern'.)* Ask the children to supply some more words containing each of these common word endings from other books.

### Vocabulary extension

**1** Choose a given number of words from the text, say ten. Ask the children to make up a wordsearch or crossword puzzle containing them. Ask them to write the clues for the crossword, or clues to be matched to the words as they are discovered in the wordsearch.

---

### Related texts:

Other books by Hazel Edwards:

'Hey Hippopotamus, Do Babies Eat Cake Too?'

'My Hippopotamus is on our Caravan Roof Getting Sunburnt'

'Stickybeak'

'There's a Hippopotamus on our Roof Eating Cake'

A story where a computer plays an important part:

'The Boggart' by Susan Cooper

## Getting Things into Perspective

### About the text

*In this explanatory text the writer explores the idea that creatures see things very differently from the way humans do.*

## Teaching opportunities at:

### TEXT Level
#### Reading comprehension

**1** Before reading, set the context of the passage by asking children to imagine they are the size of an ant. How might the world seem to them? How would a twig appear? How does a twig appear to us? Ask the children to imagine they are in a hot-air balloon, floating high in the sky. How would houses, cars and animals look? How different would they appear from the way we normally see them?

**2** Read the text to and with the class. After reading, ask the children how appropriate the title is. Does it summarise the main idea of the text? What is the main point the writer is trying to get across?

**3** Ask some specific factual questions which require children to scan the text quickly to retrieve information. *(For example, 'What light can bees see?')*

**4** Ask the children to explain why some animals have wide-angled vision. How does this help them? *(They can see all round.)*

**5** How is wide-angled vision different from binocular vision? *(Binocular vision is when both eyes see the same thing rather than different things.)*

**6** Ask the children to offer an explanation why Aborigines draw animals with backbones and internal organs showing, and why others may draw some people bigger than others to denote relative importance. Ask the children why they think the girl in the picture has such big feet.

### Writing composition

**1** Ask the children to undertake a piece of explanatory writing connected to a topic being studied in class, structured into paragraphs, with clear links between them, through the use of appropriate connectives. Remind them of the features of explanatory texts raised in the 'Grammatical awareness' section.

## SENTENCE Level
### Grammatical awareness

1 Discuss how different in style this type of information text is from a piece of narrative prose. Focus on, and find examples of, the following features in the text: a fairly formal impersonal style of writing; the presentation of facts; often written in the present tense with the passive use of verbs; the use of different examples to emphasise a point; the provision of detail; the use of diagrams or drawings.

### Sentence construction and punctuation

1 Discuss the use of brackets, inverted commas and ellipses in the text. Find examples in other pieces of writing. Review, also, the use of colons and semi-colons, dashes and hyphens by reference to examples in information books.

## WORD Level
### Spelling

1 Focus on the words 'binocular', 'telescopic', 'ultraviolet', 'aboriginal' and 'internal' in the text. Ask the children to use a dictionary to find the meaning of each. Identify the prefix in each ('bi-', 'tele-', 'ultra-', 'ab-' and 'in-') and find other words with the same prefixes. Write the meanings of these words, too.

### Vocabulary extension

1 In the same way that artists sometimes portray things not as they are in real life, so too things are not always what they seem with human relationships. What we might say and do may be two different things. The proverb 'Actions speak louder than words' sums this up. Look for examples of other proverbs and idioms. Make a class collection. Discuss what other meanings they have apart from their literal meanings.

### Related texts:

Two very interesting books:

'1001 Facts About Wild Animals' by Moira Butterfield

The second book explains how the human eye works. This would provide an excellent chance for the children to compare the piece in the passage on animal eyes with our own eye mechanism:

'How Do Our Eyes See?' by Carol Ballard

# Rules for Using the Internet

## *About the text*

*Surfing the Internet is an increasingly popular pastime, but one where rules still need to apply.*

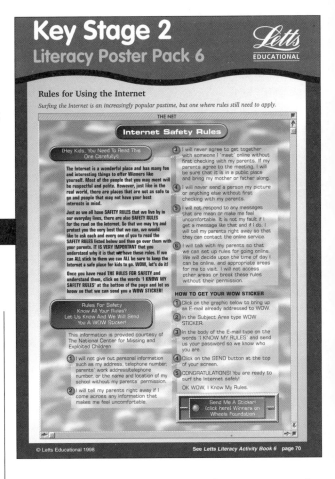

# Teaching opportunities at:

## TEXT Level
### *Reading comprehension*

**1** Ask the children to explain what the Internet is, and what 'surfing' means in this context, by way of introduction to the poster.

**2** Read the text all the way through to the class. Point out that the text has been structured in three sections. Ask the children what the main purpose is of each section. *(Why there should be safety rules – what the rules are – how to get the 'Wow' sticker.)*

**3** What is the purpose of rules? Why does it say rules are necessary? *(If appropriate, ask the children to suggest what the 'unsafe places' are and who might not 'have their best interests at heart'.)* Why does it suggest children should go over the rules with their parents? *(To agree parameters for safe use.)* What incentive does it offer for reading and understanding the rules? *(To receive a sticker.)*

**4** Why are some words in capitals and in bold? *(For emphasis and visibility.)* Are there any clues that the text comes from America? *(The spelling of 'center'.)* What evidence is there that the text is intended for children in wheelchairs? *(See the bottom of the text – WOW is an acronym for 'Winners on Wheels'.)*

**5** Read and discuss together the reason, and reasonableness, of each rule. In what way could these be considered as promises?

**6** Read the last section. In what way was the previous section a 'read and remember' section? In what way is this a 'read, understand and do' section?

## *Writing composition*

**1** Collect details of competitions being run in magazines, with products from shops, etc. Study the 'rules and conditions' accompanying them. Ask the children to invent their own competition along similar lines and write their own rules and conditions for entry.

## SENTENCE Level
### Grammatical awareness

**1** Explanatory texts often have some of the following features: a fairly formal style of writing; the presentation of facts; often written in the present tense; the passive use of verbs (e.g. 'could be seen'); the use of technical language and terms; the use of words like 'when' and 'if' to suggest what might happen; the use of charts and diagrams; a structured, step-by-step approach; the use of technical words and statistics; the provision of detail. How well does this text fit the category?

**2** Use the text to revise pronouns. How much is written in the first-person singular or plural? *(The pronouns are: 'you' [singular and plural], 'yourself' [singular], 'your' [singular and plural], 'we' [plural], 'our' [plural], 'them' [plural], 'I' [singular], 'my' [singular], 'us' [plural] and 'me' [singular].)*

### Sentence construction and punctuation

**1** Study the use of verbs in the text. Which are in the present tense? *(There are many possible answers.)* Reread the 'rules' section of the text. Note the use of the future tense and the conditional nature of much of the text (especially the use of 'if… then'). Point out the use of the imperative in the last section, and the way the text is addressed to the reader, but omits the pronoun 'you'. *(It is implicit.)*

**2** Ask the children to identify the use of connectives which help structure the text. *(For example, 'Just as', 'So that', 'However', 'If we', 'Once you', etc.)*

## WORD Level
### Spelling

**1** Find some examples of words in the text with these prefixes: 'inter-', 'in-', 're-', 'per-', 'tele-' and 'un-'.*('inter-': 'interesting', 'interests'; 'in-': 'increasingly', 'information'; 're-': 'respectful', 'respond'; 'per-': 'personal', 'permission'; 'tele-': 'telephone'; and 'un-': 'understand', 'uncomfortable'.)* Using a dictionary, find other examples of words with the same prefixes. Consider the meaning of the prefix and how it affects the meaning of the word to which it is attached.

**2** Identify and list some polysyllabic words from the text. *(There are many possible examples.)* Say them and work out how many syllables each consists of. Remind the children that where there is a double consonant, the syllable boundary falls between the consonants, e.g. 'win/ners'. Practise syllabifying the polysyllabic words and marking the syllable boundaries. Refer to dictionaries, such as 'The Concise Oxford Dictionary', to see how this is shown in them.

### Vocabulary extension

**1** Investigate some of the language associated with computers. Make up a class dictionary of computer terms, such as 'bytes', 'rams', 'chips', 'online', etc. Use some of the words collected as models and have fun making up some more 'new' words of your own.

### Related texts:

'The Internet for Kids' by Charnan Kazunas

'Kids Rule the Internet: The Ultimate Guide' by Jason Page

'The Usborne Computer Dictionary for Beginners' by Anna Claybourne

'The World Wide Web for Beginners' by Asha Kalbag

'Computers for Beginners' by Margaret Stephens

# The Machine Gunners

## About the text

*This extract, from the story by Robert Westall, is set in the Second World War. It is the first of two extracts by the same author for comparison.*

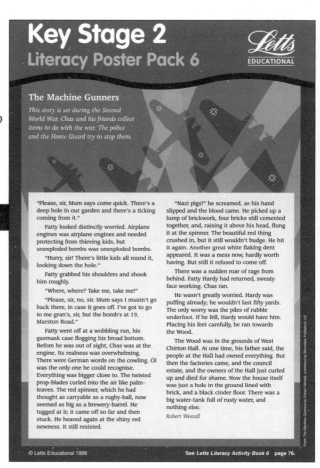

## Teaching opportunities at:

### TEXT Level
### Reading comprehension

1 Read the passage to the class. Before discussion, encourage them to respond personally to the text (see 'Writing composition').

2 Ask the children to build up a character profile of Chas from the evidence, considering his appearance, age, family, interests, character and personality, etc.

3 Now ask them to do the same for Fatty Hardy. What was he like? What did he do? What attitude did he have towards children? And so on.

4 What trick did Chas play on Fatty? Why? *(He told him there was an unexploded bomb elsewhere so he would leave the engine unguarded.)*

5 Discuss what the potential and actual dangers might be that Chas experiences during the passage. *(He faces danger from the damaged parts of the engine and from retribution by Fatty.)*

6 What evidence is there that the story is set during the Second World War? *(The introduction lets us know; also the story refers to 'Nazi pigs'.)*

7 What can be learned about 'the Wood' from the extract? *(It is in the grounds of Chirton Hall but sounds rather abandoned now. It is where Chas feels safe.)*

## Writing composition

1 After reading the text, ask the children to record their personal responses to the passage. Use the following as prompts to stimulate their responses. Did they like it? Why? Why not? What did they think of the characters? The setting? The storyline? Did the author make the story 'come alive'? Could they imagine they were there? What did they think of the author's style? His use of words and descriptive language? Would they want to read the rest of the book? Encourage an open-ended approach, rather than a question-and-answer structure to their responses.

# SENTENCE Level
## Grammatical awareness

1 Use the dialogue in the text to discuss the differences between spoken and written language. *(When we speak we often use informal language interspersed with interjections, pauses and incomplete sentences. We tend to use contractions. Speech often relies on context, and is accompanied by the use of non-verbal cues. There is no punctuation!)* Compare the dialogue with the rest of the text to reinforce these points.

2 Use the dialogue to draw attention to the use of non-standard English. *(There are many possible examples.)* Rewrite the sentences in standard English and discuss the changes that happen, for example, to the agreement of subject and verb.

## Sentence construction and punctuation

1 Find the shortest complete sentence in the text. *('Chas ran.')* Remind the children that all sentences must contain a subject and a verb. Find some other short sentences in the text and in other books and identify the subject and verb in each. Find some longer, more complex sentences. Identify the separate clauses in them and break the sentences down into shorter, single clause sentences.

2 Revise the use of apostrophes and their use for contraction and possession. Use the example, 'I've got to go to me gran's (house), sir, but the bomb's at 19, Marston Road' as a starting point.

# WORD Level
## Spelling

1 Use the verbs 'scream', 'tug', 'recognise' and 'worry' from the text. Try writing each in the present tense by adding '-s' and '-ing', and in the past tense by adding '-ed'. Note what happens (if anything) to the spelling of the root word when the suffixes are added. *('Scream': 'screams', 'screaming', 'screamed'; 'tug': 'tugs', 'tugging', 'tugged'; 'recognise': 'recognises', 'recognising', 'recognised'; 'worry': 'worries', 'worrying', 'worried'.)* Ask the children to find in the text, or think up, some other examples which fit the same patterns. Make up a rule for each set of verbs.

2 Find some examples of irregular past tenses of verbs (which don't end in '-ed') in the text and record these. *('Shook', 'went', 'was', 'were', 'stuck', 'came', 'flung', 'hit', 'fell', 'ran' and 'said'.)* Write the root verb from which each comes. *('Shake', 'go', 'be', 'be', 'are', 'stick', 'come', 'fling', 'hit', 'fall', 'run' and 'say'.)*

## Vocabulary extension

1 Investigate the use of nicknames. These may sometimes be an affectionate abbreviation of a name, for example, 'Chas' for 'Charles', or derivation of a surname, as with 'Jonesy'. Sometimes, like 'Fatty', they can refer to characteristics of a person. Discuss how these can be friendly or designed to be rather nasty.

## Related texts

'The Christmas Cat' by Robert Westall
Other 'war plane' stories:
'Biggles' by W. E. Johns
Children involved in war titles:
'Carrie's War' by Nina Bawden
'I am David' by Anne Holm
'Goodnight Mr Tom' by Michelle Magorian
'Back Home' by Michelle Magorian
'Going Back' by Penelope Lively
'No Gun for Asmir' by Christobel Mattingley
(about the Bosnian War)

# The Stones of Muncaster Cathedral

## *About the text*

*This is another extract from a book by Robert Westall. It is about a stone-mason who is restoring the spire of an old cathedral – but things don't go quite to plan.*

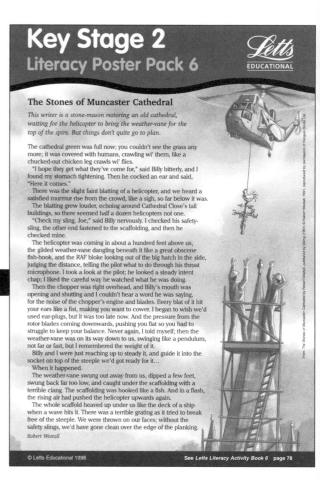

## Teaching opportunities at:

### TEXT Level
### *Reading comprehension*

**1** Read the tile and introduction and look at the illustration. Ask the children what they think could go wrong. *(Answers will depend on the children's interpretation.)*

**2** Read the text to and with the class. Were their predictions correct?

**3** What are Billy and Joe doing? *(Waiting to place the weather-vane on the spire.)* Where are they? *(On top of the cathedral.)* Why does this cause crowds to gather below? *(Discuss the vivid description of the crowds below.)*

**4** Why does Joe find his stomach 'tightening'? *(Through nervous fear and anticipation.)* Discuss the work of steeplejacks and stone-masons and some of the pleasures and hazards of the job.

**5** How do they know the helicopter is coming before it can be seen? Why call a helicopter a 'chopper'? *(Discuss the use of onomatopoeia to describe the sound it made.)*

**6** Consider how the reference to the weather-vane as 'an obscene fish-hook' has a prophetic ring to it. *(It acts as a hook when it catches the scaffolding.)*

**7** Ask the children to explain the effect the down-draught from the helicopter has on the men and on how the accident happens. *(Focus especially on the last two paragraphs.)*

**8** Ask the children to consider how the text is divided into the following sections: the introduction and setting the scene; the build-up of tension; the crisis, and how this leads the leader into the story and 'hooks' the reader.

**9** What sort of a story do the children think this is – adventure, animal, sci-fi, etc.? What do children think of the author's style and use of language? Do they like or dislike it? Find examples of good use of figurative and descriptive language. *(For example, 'like a great obscene fish-hook'. There are many possible examples.)*

## Writing composition

1 Ask the children to compare and contrast this with Unit 3.6. Use these prompts to help stimulate discussion. What type of stories are they? When do the stories take place? Who are the main characters and what are the differences in age? Are the stories told in the first- or third-person? Are they intended to be funny or serious? How well does the writer use language to set the atmosphere? Do the children like his style of writing? Which did they prefer? Why? Was there anything they didn't like about the stories?

2 The story is crying out for a resolution! Encourage the children to think about how it might continue, to draft out the next stage and to write an ending for it.

## SENTENCE Level
### Grammatical awareness

1 Find some examples of similes and discuss their use. (For example, '… humans… like a chucked-out chicken leg crawls wi' flies'.) How helpful or effective are they? Ask the children to provide some examples of common similes, or give them starters to finish in their own words, such as 'The giant was like… ', 'The bag was as heavy as… ', etc.

2 Discuss what changes would be needed if the story was rewritten in the third-person. (For example, 'Billy and I were just reaching… ' would become 'Billy and his co-worker were just reaching…') Might it lessen the drama of the passage?

### Sentence construction and punctuation

1 Try expressing some of the active sentences in the passive. (For example, 'The pressure from the rotor blades was coming downwards' becomes 'There was a downward pressure from the rotor blades'.)

## WORD Level
### Spelling

1 Ask the children to find several words in the text they find difficult. Ask them for ways of learning them. (Suggest underlining the difficult parts; saying the words as they are written; making up silly sentences or mnemonics, e.g. 'stomach' – 'Tom had a 'ch' in his stomach'; looking for smaller, known words inside each longer word; using the 'Look, say, cover, write, check' method.)

2 Select some examples of words that have been suffixed in some way. (There are many possible examples.) Identify the root word in each and what part of speech it is. How has the spelling of the root word been changed by the addition of the suffix? How has its meaning been changed?

### Vocabulary extension

1 The use of 'blatting' is particularly effective in describing the sound of the helicopter blades. Ask the children to think of other onomatopoeic words describing noises, or to make some up of their own.

2 In the book, Billy and Joe often use slang expressions. Ask the children to supply common slang words, e.g. 'scarper', 'hop it', etc. (Explain these as the sort of words we might use when we talk to each other but would generally not use when writing.)

3 Is there a local dialect in your area? Does it use words which are peculiar to the area? Investigate some of these words.

### Related texts

Other books by Robert Westall:

'The Machine Gunners'
'The Christmas Cat'

## Naming a Chinese Cat

### About the text

*This is a translation of an old Chinese fable, and is the first of two pieces, each with a cat theme.*

## Teaching opportunities at:

### TEXT Level
### Reading comprehension

**1** Look at the title, introduction and the illustration. What sort of a story is it going to be? Ask the children to explain what a fable is. *(A fable may be defined as a short story devised and written to convey a useful moral lesson.)* Ask the children to think of a good name for the cat as a way into reading the text.

**2** Ask the children why they think the old man might have called his cat Tiger.

**3** Ask the children to list the names suggested by each person in turn and the reason each gave for suggesting the name. *('Dragon' because it is mysterious; 'Cloud' because a dragon rests on clouds; 'Wind' because it blows the clouds about; 'Wall' because that holds back the wind; 'Rat' because cats kill rats.)*

**4** Ask the children to think of adjectives describing the old man's responses to the suggestions, for example, was he patient, polite? What is his final reaction? Why? *(He laughs because he has heard enough nonsense.)*

**5** What lesson can we learn from the fable? Ask the children to summarise it in one sentence. *(Don't try and make things what they are not.)*

**6** Encourage the children to read other fables, such as Aesop's fables and parables (from the Bible, for example).

**Key Stage 2**
Literacy Poster Pack 6

Letts EDUCATIONAL

**Naming a Chinese Cat**
*This story has been translated from a Chinese fable.*

Long ago in the mountains of China there lived an old man and his large family. The master of the Chi-Yen family was very fond of his large, striped ginger cat. He called it Tiger.

One day, he was outside his house, soaking up the sunshine, stroking Tiger. The cat purred contentedly on his knee. A visitor, a stranger to the village, passed by and stopped to stroke the cat. He asked its name.

'But a tiger is a wild, ferocious beast. A dragon is more mysterious. Your cat is more like a dragon. Why not change its name?' The host thanked the man and continued to stroke his cat.

Some days later, another stranger to the village saw the cat and, having heard the argument about the cat's name and character, said: 'A dragon is more mysterious than a tiger. It flies high into the sky and rests on the clouds. The clouds are therefore greater than the dragon. Why not call your cat Cloud?' The host smiled, thanked the man and watched as the cat played in the sun.

All week, people in the village dropped by, constantly changing the cat's name. One idea followed another:
'The wind blows the clouds about. Wind is the greater thing. Call your cat Wind.'
'But a wall can hold back a wind. The best name for your cat is Wall.'
'Yes, walls are strong, but they can crumble. Cats chase and kill rats. Rat is the best name for your cat, Master Chi-Yen.'

At last the old man laughed. 'Stop! Stop! Look at the animal, my friends. A cat is a cat. It lives to kill the rats in the village. It is my friend but it is also a wild beast. Listen to it howling in the night as if it were still in the jungle. Why try to change what it really is?'

© Letts Educational 1998     See *Letts Literacy Activity Book 6* page 80

### Writing composition

**1** Give the children some sayings or lessons to be learned, e.g. 'Look before you leap', 'A friend in need is a friend indeed', etc. Ask the children to make up their own fable, perhaps featuring the old man again.

**2** Play 'The Minister's Cat' game orally with the class, as a prelude to writing their own poems. The game is based on adjectives and alphabetical order. Each child in turn has to supply the next line: 'The minister's cat is an affluent cat named Arthur', 'The minister's cat is a bullying cat named Brutus', etc. When writing, encourage the use of dictionaries.

# SENTENCE Level
## Grammatical awareness

1 Find some examples of adjectives in the text. *(There are many possible examples.)* Extend the discussion to metaphors. Use the cat's names as a starter, e.g. 'The cat is like a tiger' (a simile) would become 'The cat is a tiger, prowling about, pouncing on prey', etc. Think of other animals as a basis for making up metaphors.

2 In what way could the passage be considered like a recount? *(Recounts have the following features: they contain anecdotes; they contain accounts of observations and experiences; they are usually in the first-person; they are usually written in the past tense.)*

## Sentence construction and punctuation

1 Revise the use of paragraphs. Notice how the fable is divided into paragraphs. What is the main idea of each paragraph in the text? *(For example, the old man and his cat – a visitor stops – suggests a new name for the cat – another visitor stops – suggests another name for the cat – days follow and more names are suggested – the old man laughs and keeps the cat's name as it was.)*

2 Draw attention to the way connectives are used to sequence the text, e.g. 'Long ago', 'one day', 'some days later', 'all week', etc.

# WORD Level
## Spelling

1 Write the following sentences on the board. 'The story begins in China. At the beginning the old man is outside his house'. Note that the final consonant is doubled when the suffix is added. Ask the children to add '-ing' to the following: 'permit', 'commit', 'omit', 'forget', 'refer', 'recur', 'infer', 'quarrel', 'cancel' and 'signal'. Make up a rule for what happens. *('Permitting', 'committing', 'omitting', 'forgetting', 'referring', 'quarrelling', 'cancelling', and 'signalling'. In words of more than one syllable, if the last syllable has only one vowel, we must double the last consonant before adding an ending beginning with a vowel.)*

## Vocabulary extension

1 Think of some other words associated with cats (or other animals). Use them to replace existing beginnings in words to make up some invented words, e.g. mewtaphors, clawses, purrfect, pawtable, eyetems, etc.

---

### Related texts

'The Monkey and the Water Dragon' by Joanna Troughton

'Myths and Legends from Around the World' by Sandy Shepherd

'Aesop's Fables' translated by S. A. Hanford

A set of three hilarious, modern fables:

'The Amazing Talking Pig and Other Stories' by Nick Gowar

## Macavity the Mystery Cat

Unfortunately, we have not been given permission to reproduce the illustration in poster form, which accompanies this text in Activity Book 6.

### *About the text*

*This well-known poem by T. S. Eliot is about a rather elusive cat.*

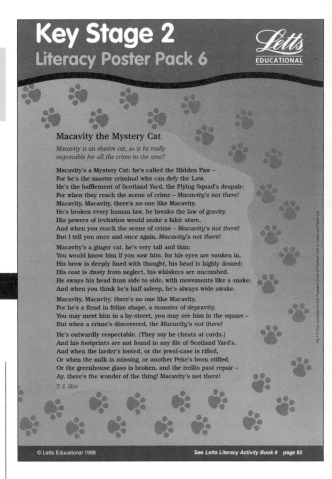

## Teaching opportunities at:

### TEXT Level
### *Reading comprehension*

**1** Read the title and introduction. Can you tell from the illustration what sort of a poem it is going to be? Why?

**2** Read the whole poem through to the class, without explaining anything. What is the poem all about? Ask the children what picture they have built up of Macavity. Why is he called a 'mystery' cat? What was the overall impact of the poem on them? Did they enjoy it? Why? What did they like or dislike about the poet's style?

**3** Which line is repeated frequently? What effect does this have? *('Macavity's not there!' – it reinforces the focus of the theme and provides the mystery.)*

**4** Ask the children to compile a profile of Macavity's physical appearance. *(He is ginger, tall and thin; his eyes are sunken, his brow lined and his head domed; his coat is dusty and his whiskers uncombed.)*

**5** What skills and attributes does he have? List these and the evidence from the poem. *(He is very agile – 'he breaks the law of gravity'; clever – 'His brow is deeply lined with thought'; deceptive – 'He's outwardly respectable'.)*

**6** What kind of crimes does he commit? *(He may cheat at cards; he steals from the larder, and takes jewellery and milk; he stifles Pekinese; and breaks glass and trellis.)*

**7** Why is he 'the Flying Squad's despair'? *(Because they cannot catch him.)*

**8** How is the poem structured? *(It is in verses, has rhyming couplets, repeating lines, rhythm, etc.)*

**9** Discuss the poet's use of language and find examples of the poet's use of figurative language, of metaphor and simile, of effective descriptive words, of alliteration. *(There are many possible examples.)*

**10** Have fun practising and performing this poem as a class.

## Writing composition

**1** Ask the children to compare this poem with Unit 3.8, 'Naming a Chinese Cat'. Use these prompts to help stimulate discussion. How are the themes similar? How do the writers treat the subject of cats – merely as animals? As animals with human characteristics? What type of texts are they? Are they written by different people? Could either be true? Are they written for different purposes (e.g. to entertain, to make you think, etc.)? Do they both tell a story or are they descriptions? Which do the children prefer? Why?

**2** Write a report for a newspaper, featuring the escapades of the 'mystery' cat and the host of unsolved crimes in the area. Think of a suitably catchy headline.

## SENTENCE Level
### Grammatical awareness

**1** Find and discuss examples of uses of the conditional in the poem. *(For example, 'You would know him if you saw him'. There are many possible examples.)*

**2** Take sentences from the poem and rewrite them, by reordering words, phrases or clauses, without changing the meaning. *(For example, 'His coat is dusty from neglect' could be written 'Macavity's coat is dusty because he neglects to wash himself'.)*

### Sentence construction and punctuation

**1** Revise different punctuation marks by reference to the text. Ask the children to identify specific marks and to explain their functions. *(Apostrophes for contraction and possession, colons to separate clauses, dashes as strong commas, commas for lists, exclamation marks for emphasis, semi-colons for pauses, and full stops.)*

## WORD Level
### Spelling

**1** Hold a 'letter pattern' hunt. Provide the children with a range of letter patterns, e.g. 'aw', 'sc', 'ough', etc. Ask them to find as many words as possible containing each letter pattern in the text. *(For example, 'law', 'Scotland', 'thought'.)* Compare the words in each set. Are the letter patterns in each word pronounced the same? Can each set be further sub-divided? Ask the children to add further examples of words from other books containing each letter pattern.

### Vocabulary extension

**1** Choose some words from the text that have been prefixed or suffixed. *(There are many possible examples.)* Change the prefix or suffix in each word and have fun making some new words, e.g. 'bafflement' – 'bafflation'; 'respectable' – 'inspectable', etc.

### Related texts

Other books by T. S. Eliot:

'Growltiger's Last Stand'

'The Illustrated Old Possum'

'Old Possum's Book of Practical Cats'

'Mr Mistoffolees with Mungojerrie and Rumpelteazer'

'The House of a Hundred Cats' by Irene Rawnsley

## The BT Tower

### *About the text*

*This is an excample of a factual information text, promoting the B.T. Tower.*

# Teaching opportunities at:

## TEXT Level
### *Reading comprehension*

**1** Look at the title, the introduction and the picture of the BT Tower. Ask if any children have seen it and encourage their anecdotal experiences. Ask if any children have been up any very tall buildings and encourage them to describe their experiences and feelings.

**2** Before reading the text to the class, ask the children to look quickly at the sub-headings. Ask them in which section they would expect to find specific information, e.g. on the restaurant. *(In this case, 'Food for thought'.)* Ask them to scan the text quickly to see who can find the following information the quickest: when the tower opened; how long it takes the top to revolve in a complete circle, etc.

**3** Read the whole text to the class and ask them to give the gist of it in general terms. What is its purpose? Who might it have been written for? How interesting is it? What value does it have? How successful was it in persuading them that it is an interesting building worth seeing? How did it achieve this?

**4** Is it best described as an information, promotional or an advertising leaflet? What governed their choice?

**5** Close-read each section again, one at a time and ask specific questions requiring literal and inferential comprehension based on the information. *(For example, 'How long do the lifts take to get to the top?')*

### *Writing composition*

**1** Encourage the children to develop their note-taking skills by filleting each paragraph, noting key words and phrases.

**2** Ask the children to produce a slick, punchy advertising poster for the BT Tower using only a given number of words and illustrations.

**3** Ask the children to write a short promotional leaflet for your town. Link this with work done under 'Grammatical awareness' using the features detailed as an *aide-memoire*.

# SENTENCE Level
## Grammatical awareness

1 Ask the children to suggest what persuasive techniques the leaflet uses, such as humour, mystery, pictures, the presentation of facts and figures in an interesting way, the use of powerful language, arousing curiosity, etc.

2 Discuss the following features of some information leaflets: subheadings; use of bold print; use of bullet points; use of third-person; passive verbs; present tense; presentation of facts and figures and some technical terms; and clearly structured sections. Which does this leaflet contain?

## Sentence construction and punctuation

1 Reread the BT Tower text and notice that it is very much written in an impersonal voice. Ask the children to imagine they have visited the Tower and ask them to use the same information, but write it as a recount of their visit and what they have discovered. Compare the results, noting the prominence of the personal voice in the recounted version.

# WORD Level
## Spelling

1 Identify and list some polysyllabic words from the text. *(There are many possible examples.)* Say them and work out how many syllables each consists of. Remind children that where there is a double consonant, the syllable boundary falls between the consonants, e.g. 'shil/ling'. Practise syllabifying the polysyllabic words and marking in syllable boundaries. Refer to dictionaries such as 'The Concise Oxford Dictionary' that show the syllabification of words and explain the marking conventions they use. Consider which of the syllables are stressed and unstressed in the words.

2 Ask the children to volunteer some tricky words from the extract, such as 'characteristic'. Ask the children for suggestions on how they could remember them. *(Suggest underlining the difficult parts; saying the words as they are written; making up silly sentences or mnemonics; looking for smaller, known words inside each longer word; using the 'Look, say, cover, write, check' method.)*

## Vocabulary extension

1 Select a number of interesting words from the passage, for example, 'microwave', and ask the children to write definitions for them. Then give the children some definitions of words (and not the words themselves), and ask them to find the words they refer to in the text, cross-checking their guesses in their own dictionaries. Encourage the children to carry out the same exercise. They should choose some difficult words between themselves, find and write definitions for them, and give the definitions only to a partner to match with the correct words in the text.

## Related texts

'The Usborne Book of London' by Moira Butterfield
'London' by Gill Harvey
'Look Out London' by Louise Nicholson
'How They Were Built' by David J. Brown
'The Fantastic Cutaway Book of Giant Buildings' by J. Kirkwood

# Handy Hints for Writing a Book Review

**You must:**
- Explain to others what the book is about.
- Make them so interested they want to read it themselves.

**Title and author**
- Give information so others can find the book.

**Setting**
- Say where and when the story or events took place.

**Plot**
- Say what happens in the story.
- Do not give away the ending!

**Characters**
- Say who the main characters are.
- What are they like?
  - how do they behave?        – what do they say?
  - what do they look like?
- How do you feel about them?
  - do your feelings change?      – why?

**Finally**
- Say why you enjoyed the book.
Always give your reasons.

# Handy Hints for Planning Stories

## SETTING

● Where will your story take place?

- in a house?
- in a shop?
- in a wood?
- in a castle?
- in a hospital?
- in a cave?
- at the seaside?
- at school?
- at a fair?
- somewhere else?

## CHARACTERS

● Who will be in your story?

- will they be humans?
- will they be animals?
- will they be monsters?
- will they be something else?

● What will they look like?

● What sort of things will they do?

● What sort of things will they say?

## STORYLINE

● What will your story be about?

● How will it begin?

● What sort of things will happen in the middle?

● How will your story end?

- happily?
- sadly?
- amusingly?
- will you make it into a 'cliffhanger', leaving the reader wanting to know more?

# Handy Hints for Handwriting

## BEFORE YOU BEGIN

- Are you sitting comfortably?
- Are you sitting up straight?
- Have you got enough light?
- Have you got a smooth surface to write on?
- Have you sloped your paper slightly?
- Have you got a suitable pen or pencil to write with?
- Are you holding your pen or pencil in a comfortable way?
- Can you see what you are writing?

## WHEN YOU HAVE FINISHED

- Is the writing neat?
- Is it easy to read?
- Does it 'sit' on the line?
- Are all letters well shaped?
- Are the letters evenly sized?
- Are any letters too tall or too small?
- Are the descenders of any letters too long or curly?
- Is there enough space between the words and letters?
- Are all the joins well made?
- Have you put capital letters in all the correct places?
- Have you used punctuation marks correctly?

# Handy Hints for Checking Your Writing

## SENTENCES
- Do your sentences make sense?
- Is there anything you want to move or change?
- Is there anything you can leave out to make it clearer?

## PUNCTUATION
- Have you punctuated it correctly with:
  - capital letters, full stops, question marks, exclamation marks, speech marks and commas?

## SPELLING
- Have you checked for silly spelling mistakes?
- Have you looked up any words you are not sure of?

## HANDWRITING
- Is your handwriting easy to read?
- Or are you going to do your work on the computer?

## PRESENTATION
- Have you thought of a good title?
- Are you going to illustrate your work?
  - what sort of illustrations would be best? (pictures, diagrams, etc.)
  - where will you place the illustrations?
- In what form will you present your work?
  - in an exercise book?
  - on paper?
  - as a zig-zag concertina book?
  - in some other format?

# Handy Hints for Using Punctuation Marks (1)

**Punctuation** helps us make sense of what we read.
**Punctuation marks** make writing easier for us to understand.
They help us to read with expression.

### Full stop
A **full stop** tells you to stop. You have come to the end of a sentence.
Every sentence must begin with a capital letter.
The dog chased the postman.

### Question mark
A **question mark** tells you a question is being asked.
What is the time?

### Comma
A **comma** tells you to pause.  It is also used to separate items in a list.
After eating his dinner, the old man had a sleep.
In her bag Mrs Jones had apples, pears, bananas and grapes.

### Exclamation mark
An exclamation mark is used when we feel strongly about something or are surprised.
Stop that thief!

### Speech marks
We use **speech marks** to show someone is speaking.
We write what the person says inside the speech marks.
Tom said, "I like to watch television in the evening."

# Handy Hints for Using Punctuation Marks (2)

## Apostrophe
An **apostrophe** is like a raised comma. It is used in two ways:

1. In **contractions** (when words are shortened by leaving out letters). The apostrophe shows something has been missed out.

For example, **do not** can be written as **don't**

2. It can be used to show **possession**.

– the book belonging to the girl = **the girl's book**

– the book belonging to the girls = **the girls' book**

## Colon
A **colon** is often used to introduce a list, before someone speaks, or instead of a full stop.

He was very cold: the temperature was below zero.

The fridge contained: eggs, butter, milk and yoghurt.

Louise said: "What are you doing here?"

## Semi-colon
A **semi-colon** is a punctuation mark used to separate parts of a sentence. It is stronger than a comma but not as strong as a full stop.

Sam loves Indian food; Tom prefers Italian food.

## Dash
A **dash** holds words apart. It is stronger than a comma, but not as strong as a full stop.

There is only one meal worth eating – spaghetti!

## Hyphen
**Hyphens** link words together.     I love freshly-baked bread.

## Brackets
**Brackets** can be used like dashes. They can separate off part of a sentence or put in an extra example:

He was awarded a prize in school (not before time)

# Other Literacy Materials available from Letts Educational:

Reception *Poster Pack* and *Teacher's Book*
Year 1 *Poster Pack* and *Teacher's Book*

Year 2 Term 1 *Activity Book*
Year 2 Term 2 *Activity Book*
Year 2 Term 3 *Activity Book*

Year 2 *Poster Pack* and *Teacher's Book*

Year 3 *Activity Book*
Year 4 *Activity Book*
Year 5 *Activity Book*
Year 6 *Activity Book*

Year 3 *Poster Pack* and *Teacher's Book*
Year 4 *Poster Pack* and *Teacher's Book*
Year 5 *Poster Pack* and *Teacher's Book*
Year 6 *Poster Pack* and *Teacher's Book*

## *Coming soon:*

Year 3 *Differentiated Activity Book – Sentence Level*
Year 3 *Differentiated Activity Book – Word Level*

Year 4 *Differentiated Activity Book – Sentence Level*
Year 4 *Differentiated Activity Book – Word Level*

Year 5 *Differentiated Activity Book – Sentence Level*
Year 5 *Differentiated Activity Book – Word Level*

Year 6 *Differentiated Activity Book – Sentence Level*
Year 6 *Differentiated Activity Book – Word Level*

For more information or a catalogue request call **Freephone 0800 216592**